Pokémon Adventures™

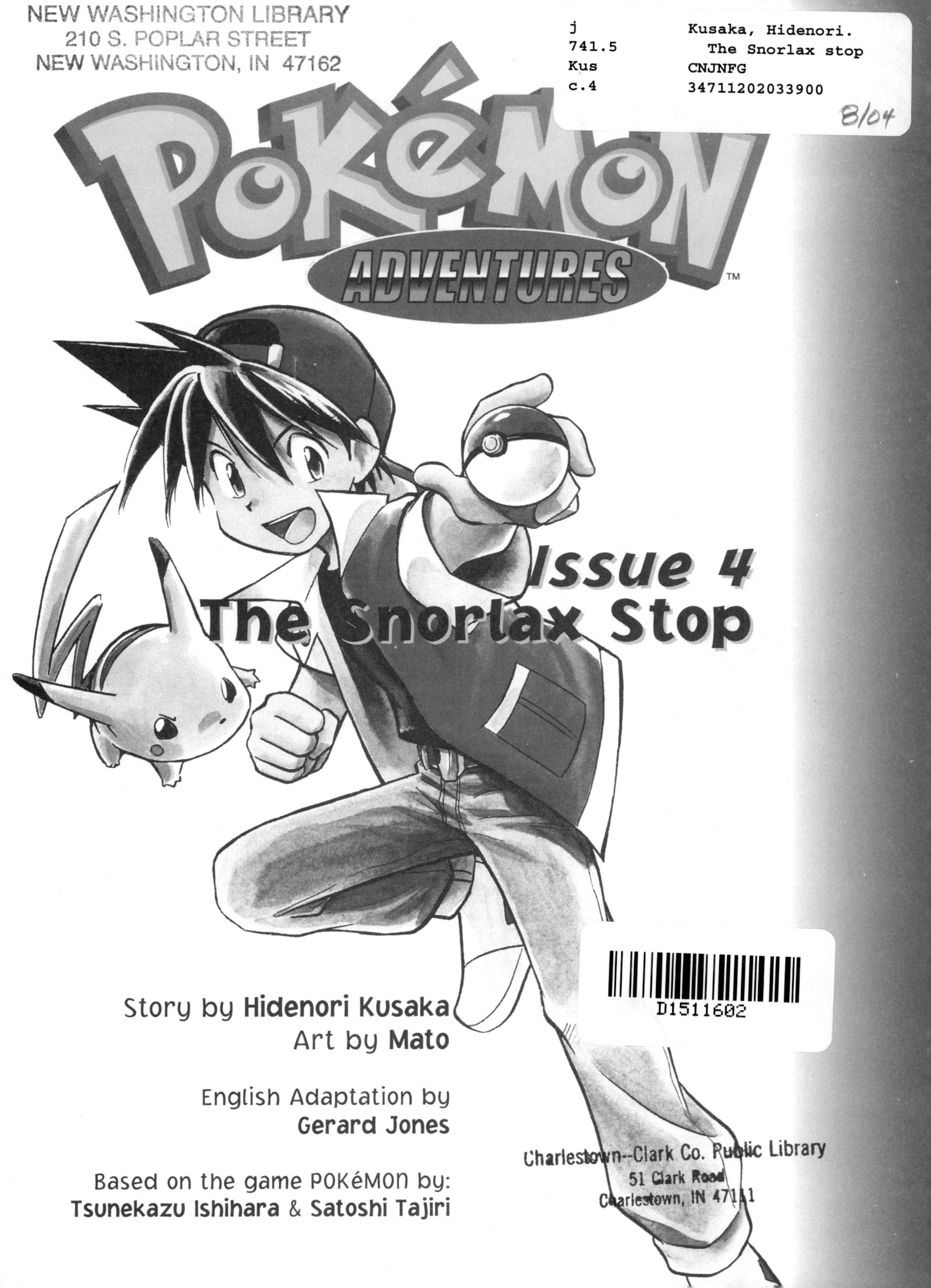

Issue 4
The Snorlax Stop

Story by **Hidenori Kusaka**
Art by **Mato**

English Adaptation by
Gerard Jones

Based on the game POKéMON by:
Tsunekazu Ishihara & **Satoshi Tajiri**

POKéMON ADVENTURES
Issue 4:
The Snorlax Stop

Story/Hidenori Kusaka
Art/Mato

English Adaptation/Gerard Jones

Translation/Kaori Inoue
Touch-up & Lettering/Dan Nakrosis
Graphics & Design/Carolina Ugalde
Editing/William Flanagan

Editor-in-Chief/Hyoe Narita
Publisher/Seiji Horibuchi

First published by
Shogakukan, Inc. in Japan.

Published by Viz Comics
P.O. Box 77064
San Francisco, CA 94107

For advertising opportunities, call:
Oliver Chin
Director of Sales and Marketing
(415) 546-7073 ext. 128

Ask for our **free**
Viz Shop-By-Mail catalog!

Call toll free: (800) 394-3042
Or visit us on-line at our web site:
www.viz.com. And check out our
internet magazines: www.j-pop.com
and www.animerica-mag.com & get
your free Viz e-mail newsletter!

CONTENT

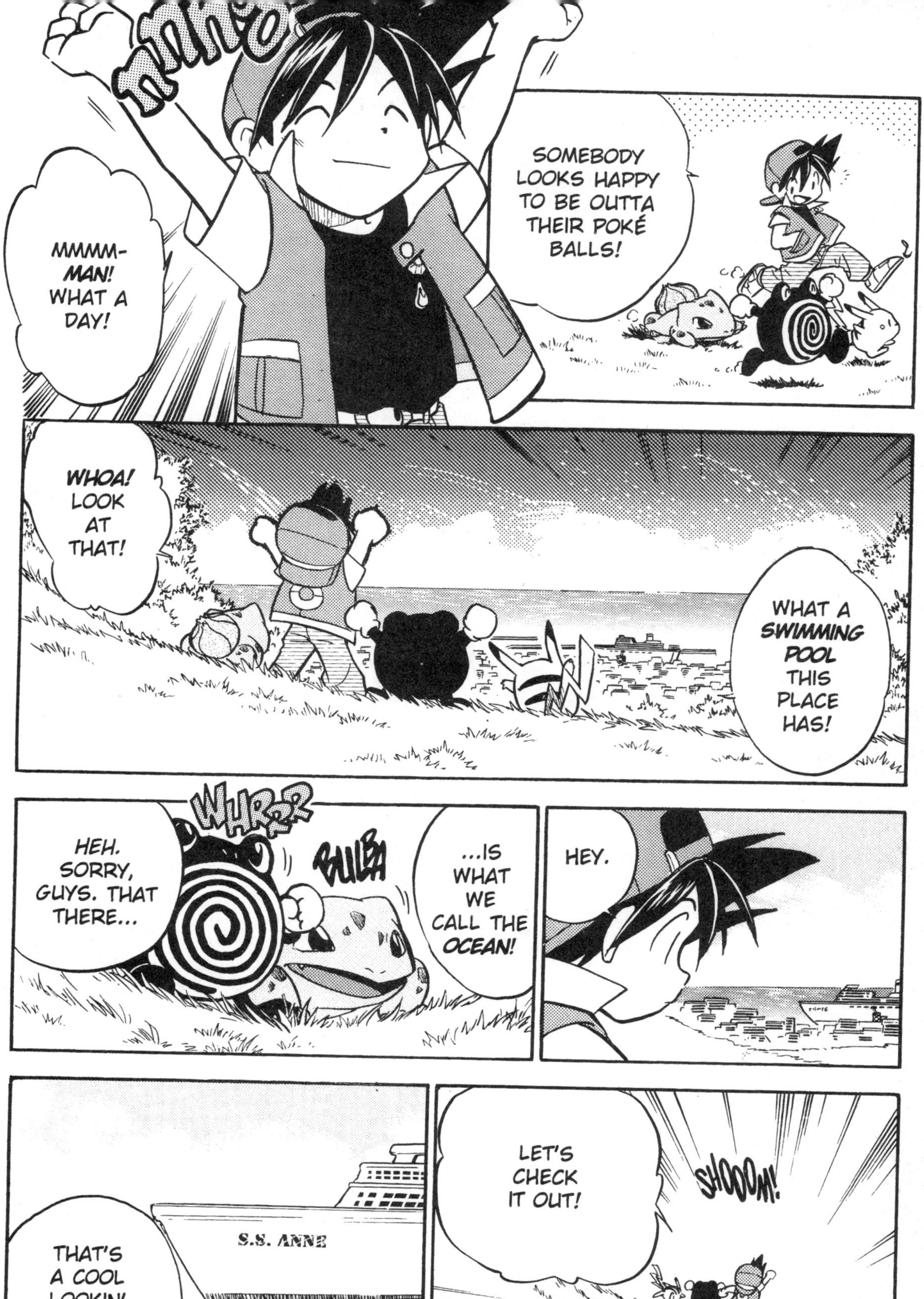
MMMM-MAN! WHAT A DAY!
SOMEBODY LOOKS HAPPY TO BE OUTTA THEIR POKÉ BALLS!
WHOA! LOOK AT THAT!
WHAT A SWIMMING POOL THIS PLACE HAS!
WHRRR
HEH. SORRY, GUYS. THAT THERE...
BULBA
...IS WHAT WE CALL THE OCEAN!
HEY.
S.S. ANNE
THAT'S A COOL LOOKIN' SHIP...
LET'S CHECK IT OUT!
SHOOOM!

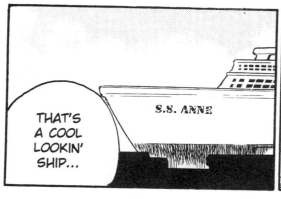

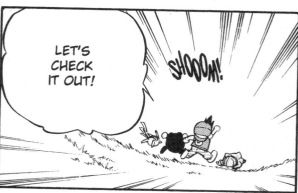

10 DANGER: HIGH VOLTORB

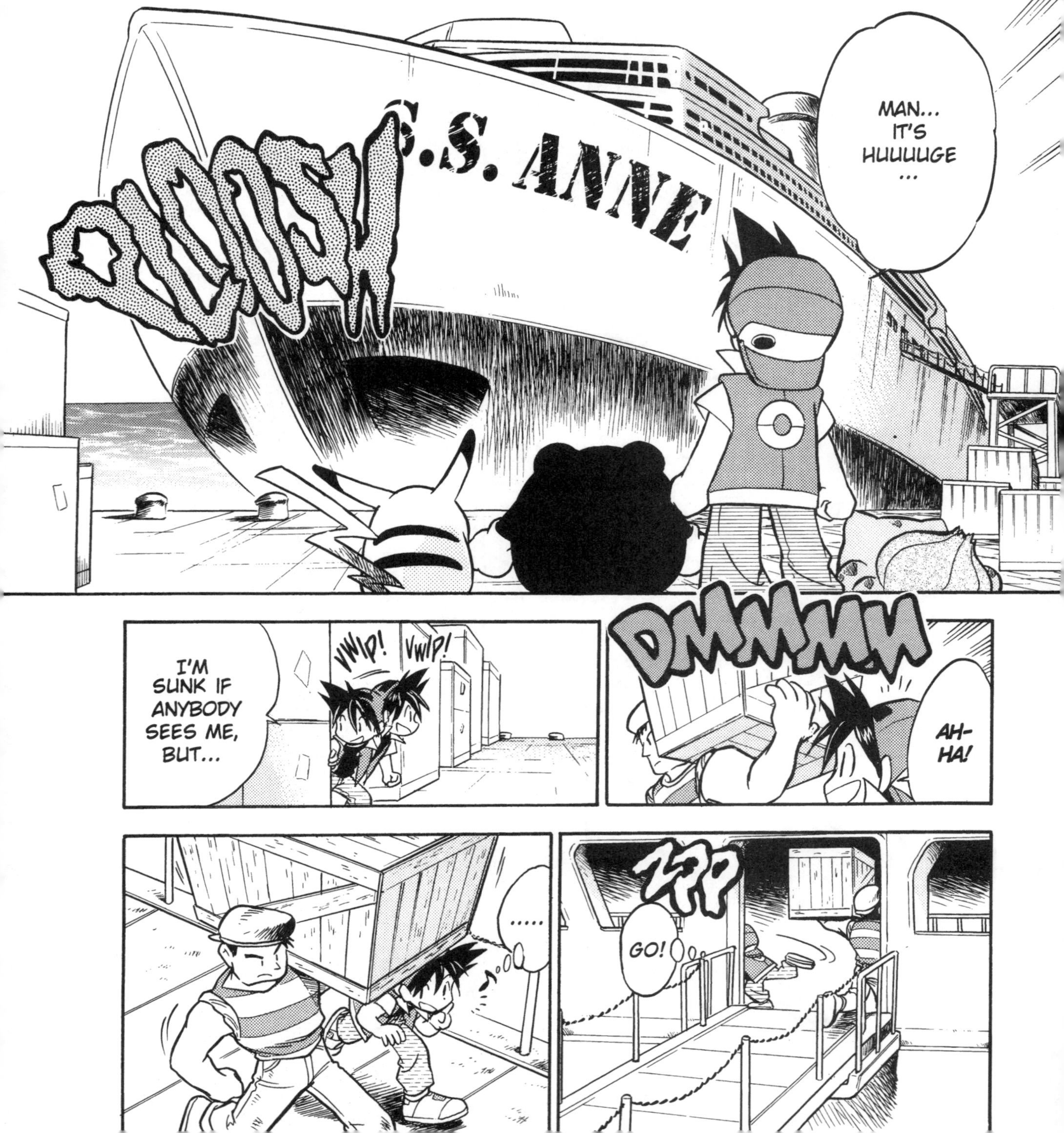

BLOOOSH
S.S. ANNE
MAN... IT'S HUUUUGE...
I'M SUNK IF ANYBODY SEES ME, BUT...
VWIP! VWIP!
AH-HA!
.....
GO!

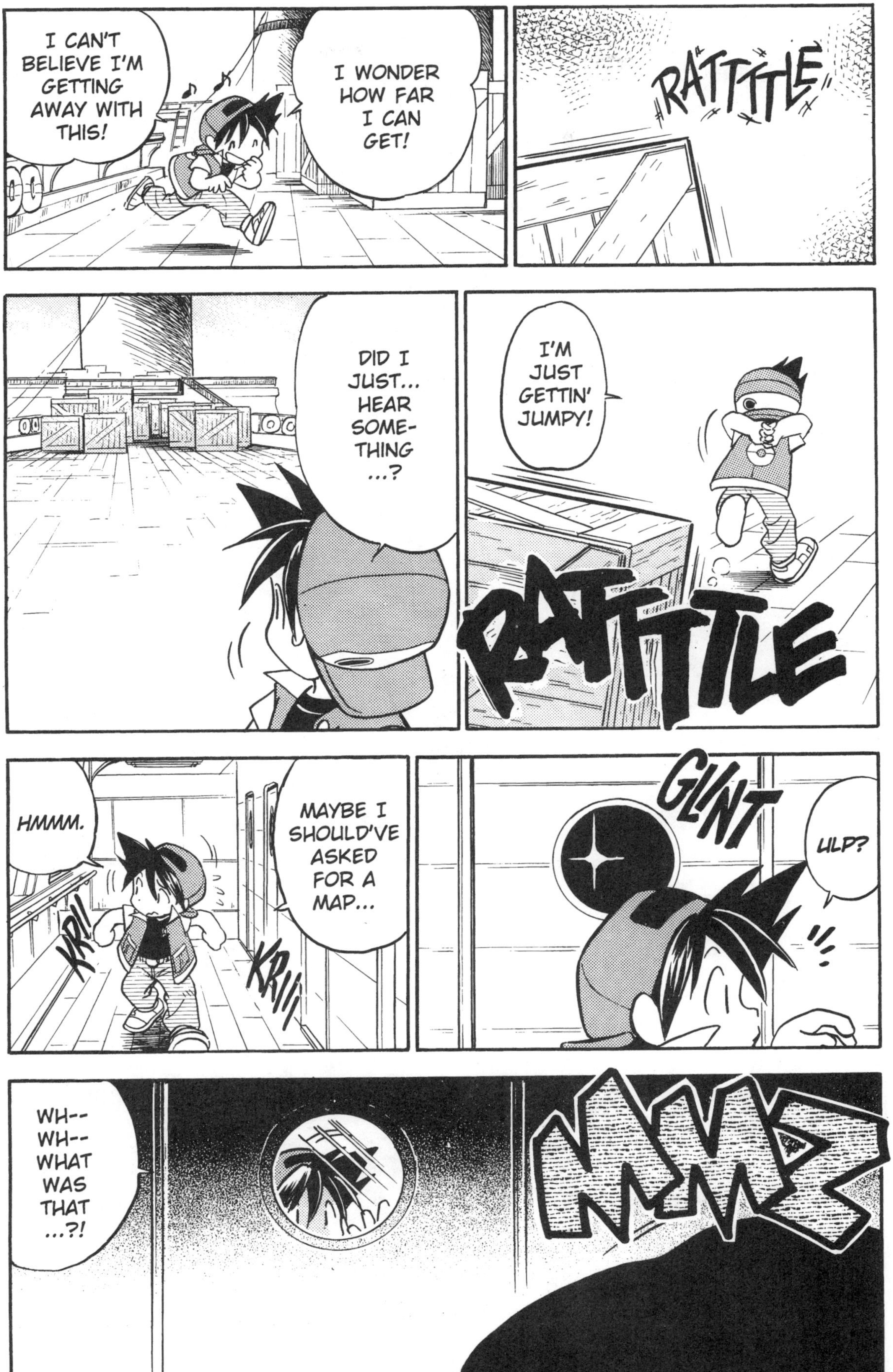
I CAN'T BELIEVE I'M GETTING AWAY WITH THIS!
I WONDER HOW FAR I CAN GET!
RATTTTLE
DID I JUST... HEAR SOME-THING ...?
I'M JUST GETTIN' JUMPY!
RATTTLE
HMMM.
KRI!
MAYBE I SHOULD'VE ASKED FOR A MAP...
KRI!!
GLINT
ULP?
WH-- WH-- WHAT WAS THAT ...?!

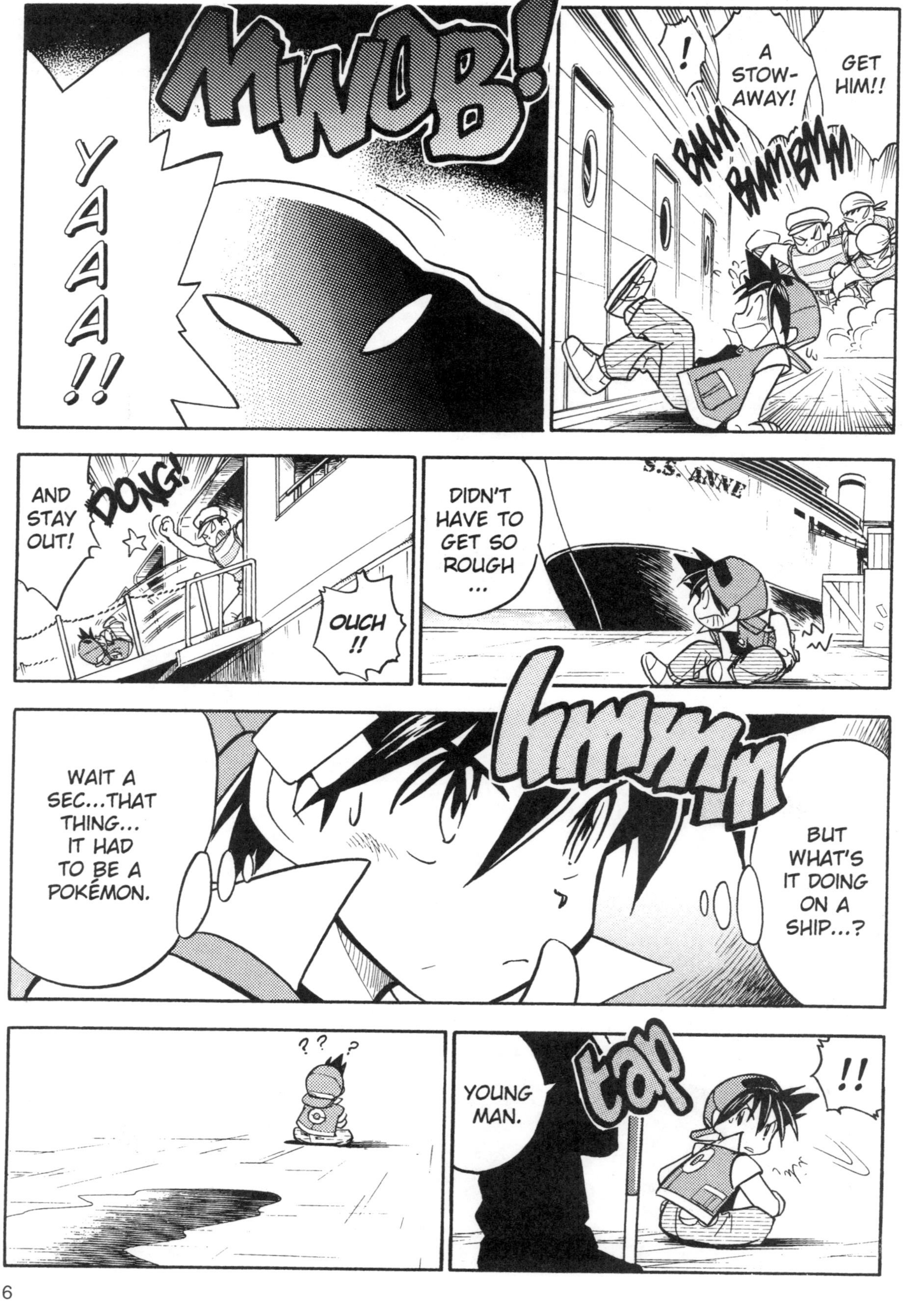
MWOB!
YAAAA!!
!
A STOW-AWAY!
GET HIM!!
BAM BAMBAM
AND STAY OUT!
DONG!
OUCH!!
S.S. ANNE
DIDN'T HAVE TO GET SO ROUGH...
hmmmn
WAIT A SEC...THAT THING... IT HAD TO BE A POKÉMON.
BUT WHAT'S IT DOING ON A SHIP...?
???
YOUNG MAN.
tap
!!

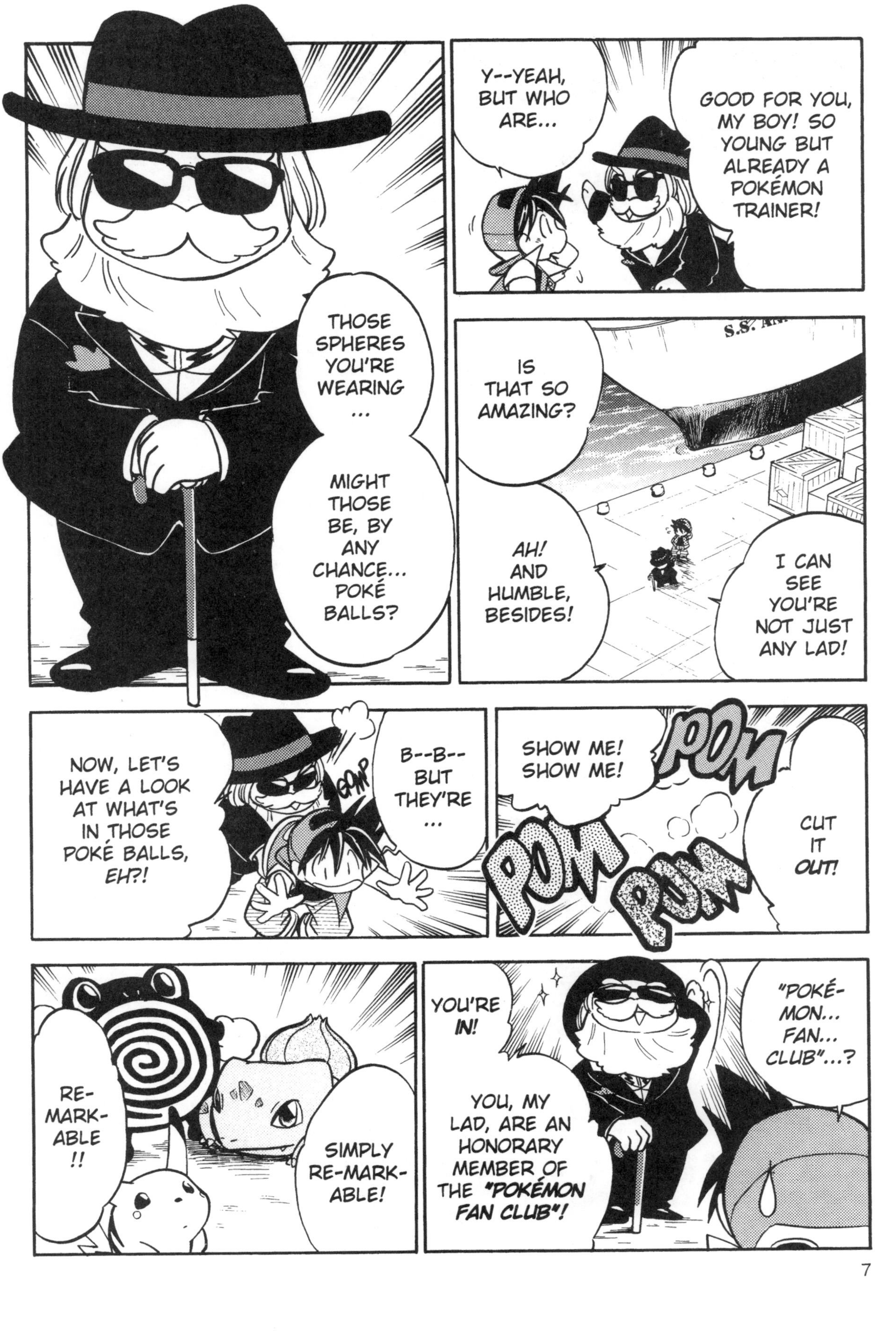

THOSE SPHERES YOU'RE WEARING ...
MIGHT THOSE BE, BY ANY CHANCE... POKÉ BALLS?
Y--YEAH, BUT WHO ARE...
GOOD FOR YOU, MY BOY! SO YOUNG BUT ALREADY A POKÉMON TRAINER!
S.S.
IS THAT SO AMAZING?
AH! AND HUMBLE, BESIDES!
I CAN SEE YOU'RE NOT JUST ANY LAD!
NOW, LET'S HAVE A LOOK AT WHAT'S IN THOSE POKÉ BALLS, EH?!
B--B-- BUT THEY'RE ...
SHOW ME! SHOW ME!
POM
POM
POM
CUT IT OUT!
RE-MARK-ABLE !!
SIMPLY RE-MARK-ABLE!
YOU'RE IN!
YOU, MY LAD, ARE AN HONORARY MEMBER OF THE "POKÉMON FAN CLUB"!
"POKÉ-MON... FAN... CLUB"...?

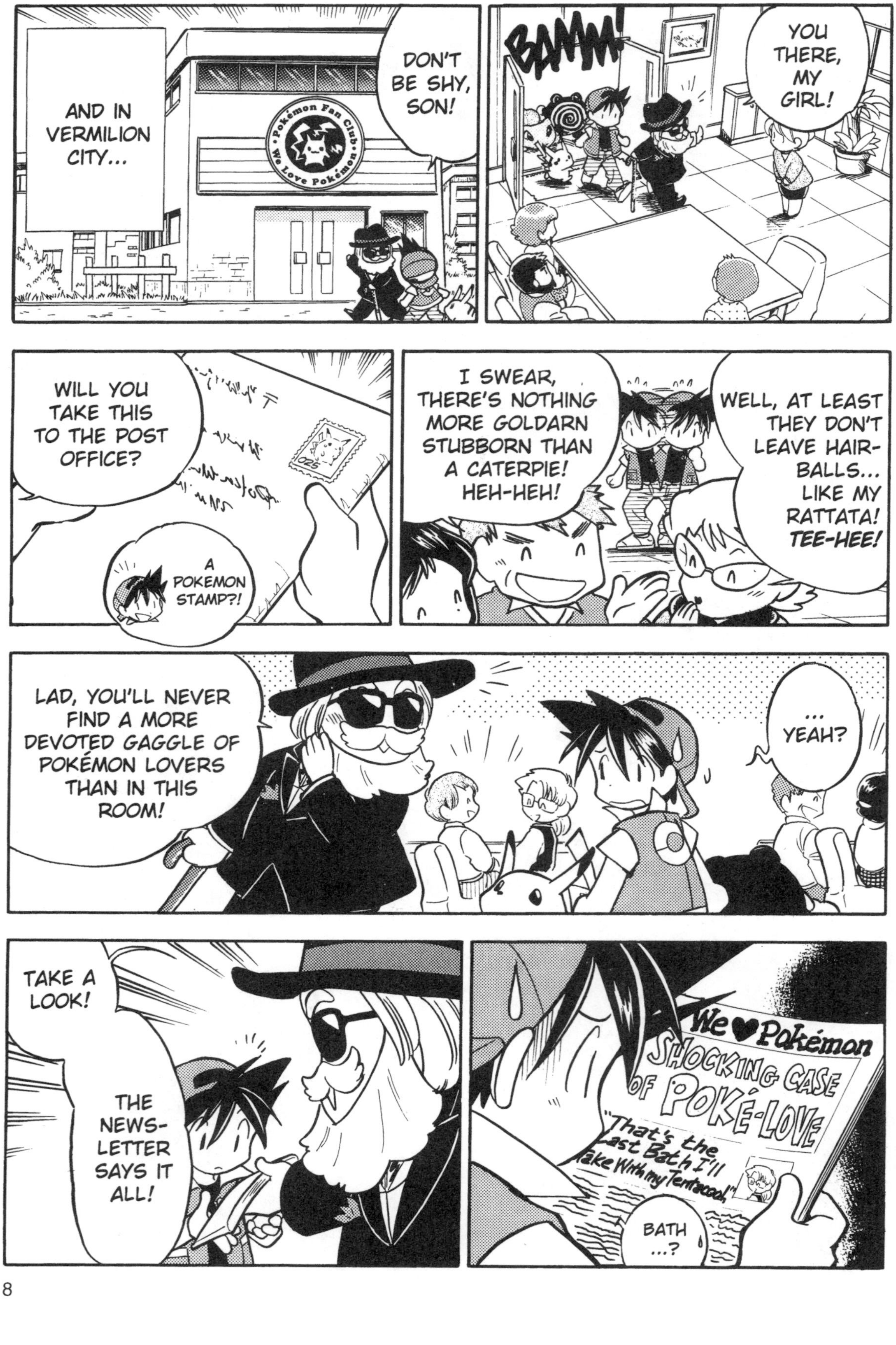
AND IN VERMILION CITY...
Pokémon Fan Club
We Love Pokémon
DON'T BE SHY, SON!
BAMM!
YOU THERE, MY GIRL!
WILL YOU TAKE THIS TO THE POST OFFICE?
025
A POKEMON STAMP?!
I SWEAR, THERE'S NOTHING MORE GOLDARN STUBBORN THAN A CATERPIE! HEH-HEH!
WELL, AT LEAST THEY DON'T LEAVE HAIR-BALLS... LIKE MY RATTATA! TEE-HEE!
LAD, YOU'LL NEVER FIND A MORE DEVOTED GAGGLE OF POKÉMON LOVERS THAN IN THIS ROOM!
... YEAH?
TAKE A LOOK!
THE NEWS-LETTER SAYS IT ALL!
We ♥ Pokémon
SHOCKING CASE OF POKÉ-LOVE
"That's the Last Bath I'll Take With my Tentacool!"
BATH ...?

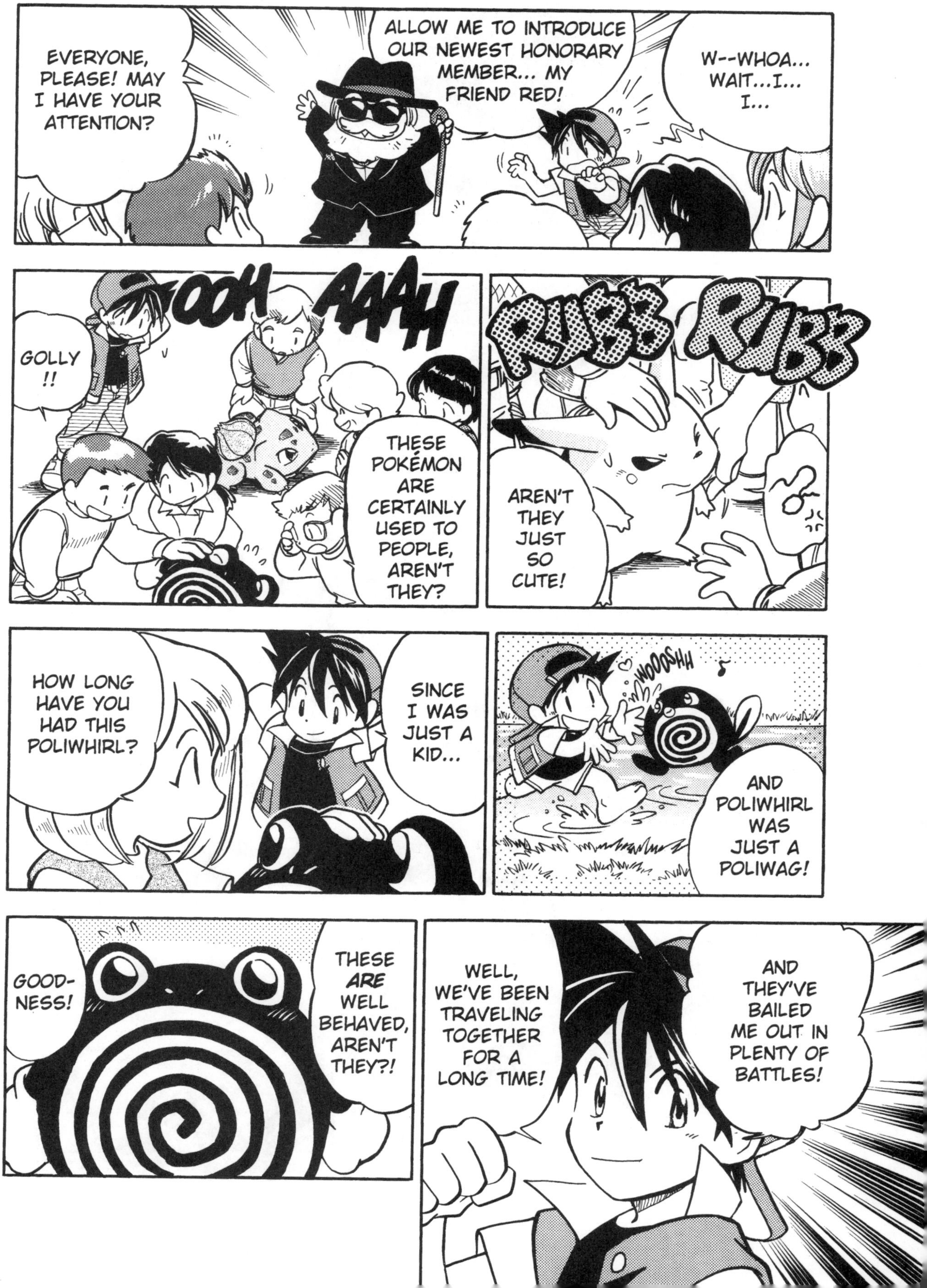
EVERYONE, PLEASE! MAY I HAVE YOUR ATTENTION?
ALLOW ME TO INTRODUCE OUR NEWEST HONORARY MEMBER... MY FRIEND RED!
W--WHOA... WAIT...I... I...
OOH
AAAH
GOLLY !!
THESE POKÉMON ARE CERTAINLY USED TO PEOPLE, AREN'T THEY?
RUBB RUBB
AREN'T THEY JUST SO CUTE!
HOW LONG HAVE YOU HAD THIS POLIWHIRL?
SINCE I WAS JUST A KID...
WOOOSHH
AND POLIWHIRL WAS JUST A POLIWAG!
GOOD-NESS!
THESE *ARE* WELL BEHAVED, AREN'T THEY?!
WELL, WE'VE BEEN TRAVELING TOGETHER FOR A LONG TIME!
AND THEY'VE BAILED ME OUT IN PLENTY OF BATTLES!

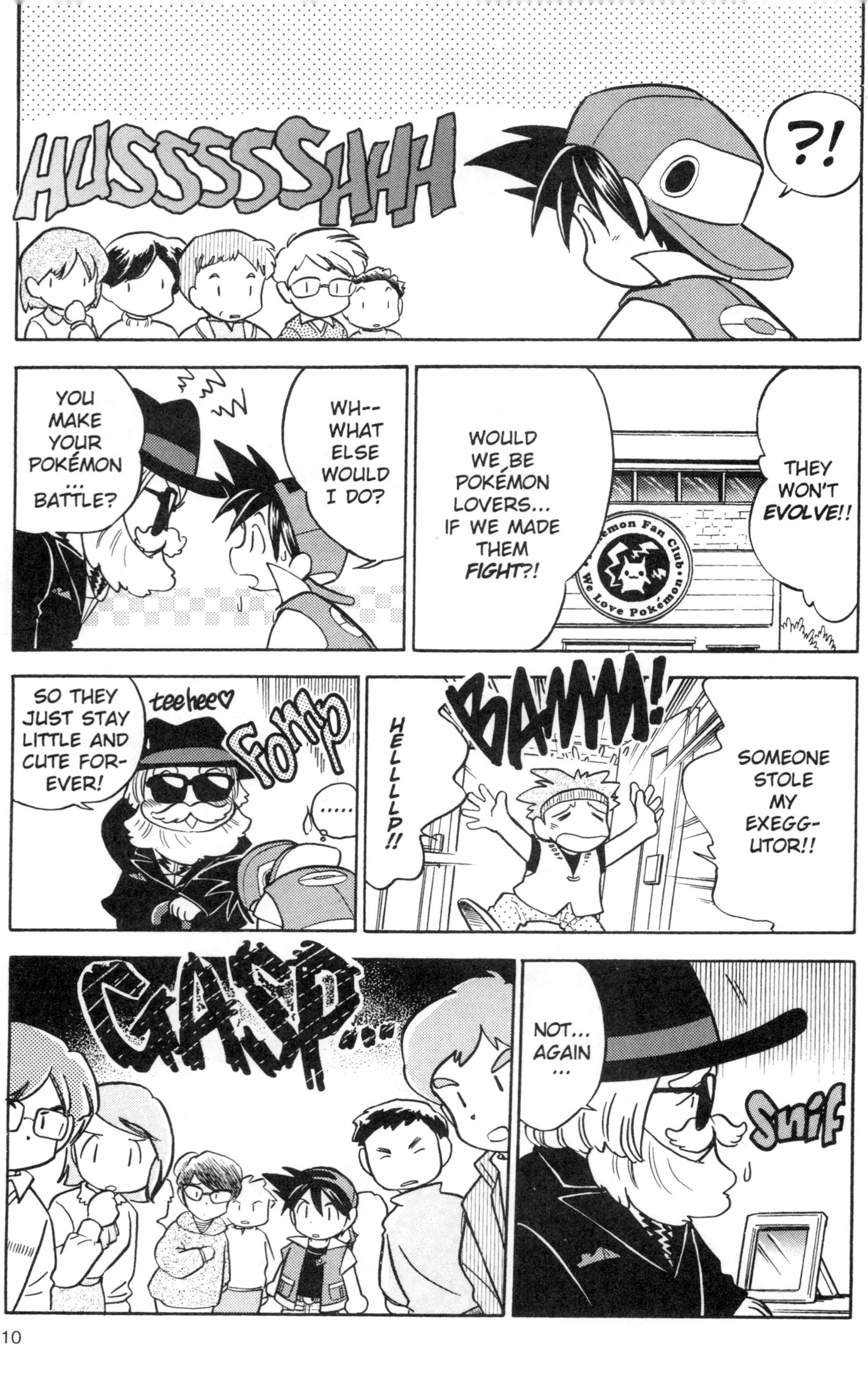
HUSSSSHHH
?!
YOU MAKE YOUR POKÉMON ... BATTLE?
WH-- WHAT ELSE WOULD I DO?
WOULD WE BE POKÉMON LOVERS... IF WE MADE THEM FIGHT?!
We Love Pokémon
THEY WON'T EVOLVE!!
SO THEY JUST STAY LITTLE AND CUTE FOR-EVER!
teehee♡
Fomp
......
BAMM!
HELLLLP!!
SOMEONE STOLE MY EXEGG-UTOR!!
GASP...
NOT... AGAIN ...
Snif

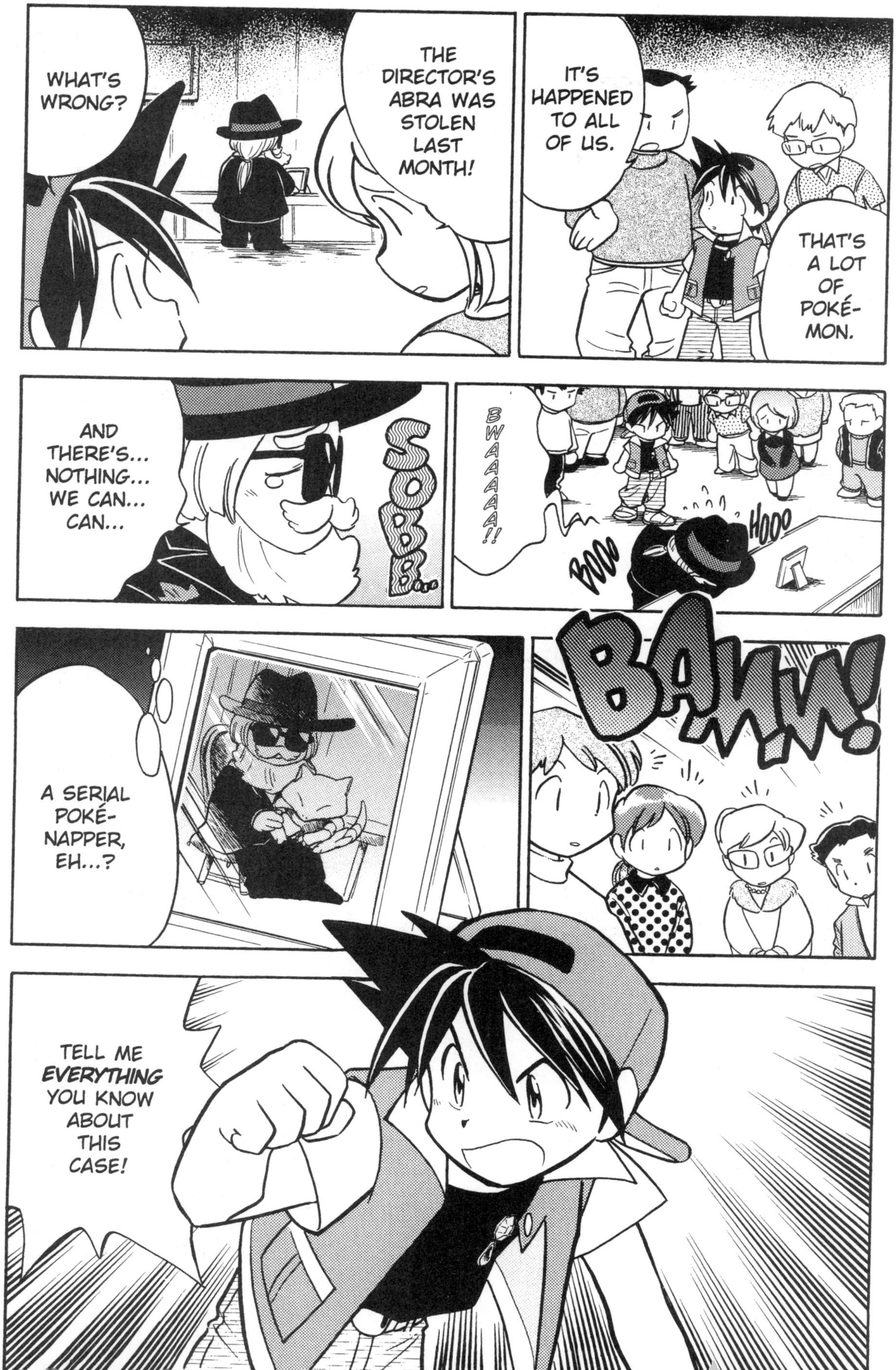
WHAT'S WRONG?
THE DIRECTOR'S ABRA WAS STOLEN LAST MONTH!
IT'S HAPPENED TO ALL OF US.
THAT'S A LOT OF POKÉ-MON.
AND THERE'S... NOTHING... WE CAN... CAN...
SOBBB...
BWAAAAAAA!!
HOOO
BOOO
A SERIAL POKÉ-NAPPER, EH...?
BAMM!
TELL ME **EVERYTHING** YOU KNOW ABOUT THIS CASE!

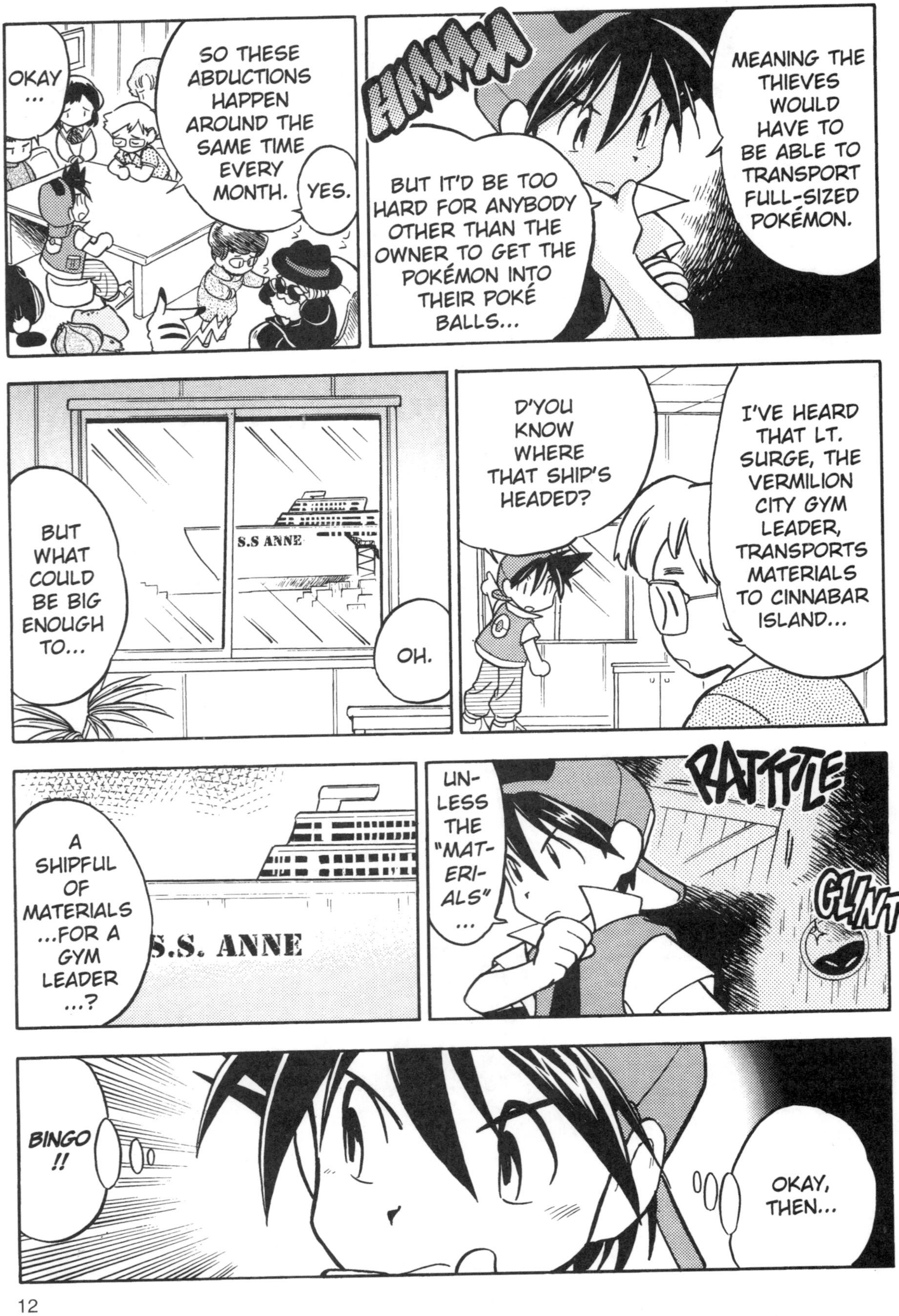
OKAY ...
SO THESE ABDUCTIONS HAPPEN AROUND THE SAME TIME EVERY MONTH.
YES.
HMMM
BUT IT'D BE TOO HARD FOR ANYBODY OTHER THAN THE OWNER TO GET THE POKÉMON INTO THEIR POKÉ BALLS...
MEANING THE THIEVES WOULD HAVE TO BE ABLE TO TRANSPORT FULL-SIZED POKÉMON.
BUT WHAT COULD BE BIG ENOUGH TO...
S.S ANNE
OH.
D'YOU KNOW WHERE THAT SHIP'S HEADED?
I'VE HEARD THAT LT. SURGE, THE VERMILION CITY GYM LEADER, TRANSPORTS MATERIALS TO CINNABAR ISLAND...
A SHIPFUL OF MATERIALS ...FOR A GYM LEADER ...?
S.S. ANNE
UN-LESS THE "MAT-ERI-ALS" ...
RATTTLE
GLINT
BINGO !!
OKAY, THEN...

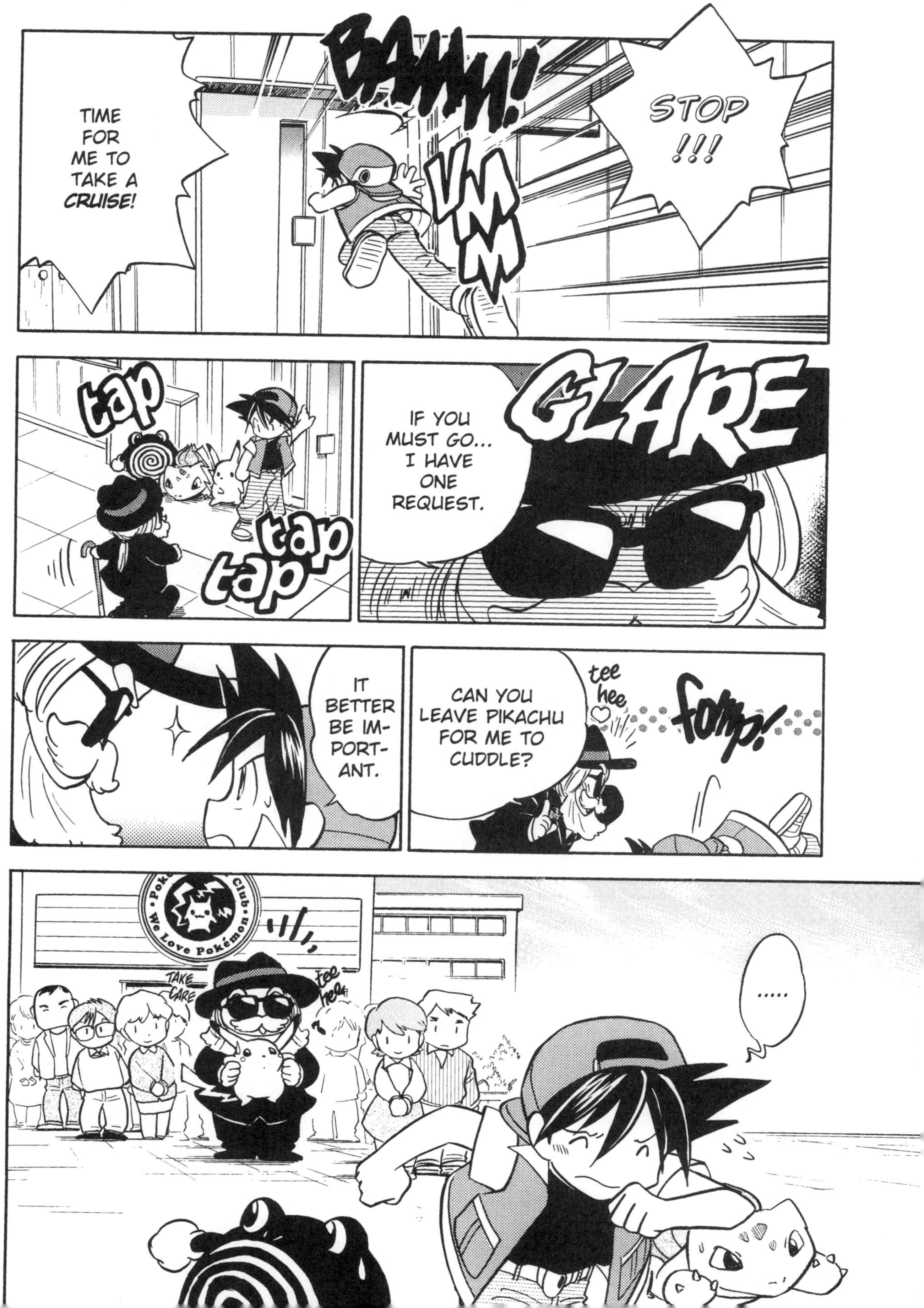
TIME FOR ME TO TAKE A CRUISE!
BAMMM!
VMMM
STOP!!!
tap
tap tap
IF YOU MUST GO... I HAVE ONE REQUEST.
GLARE
IT BETTER BE IM-PORT-ANT.
CAN YOU LEAVE PIKACHU FOR ME TO CUDDLE?
tee hee
fomp!
Club
We Love Pokémon
TAKE CARE
tee hee
.....

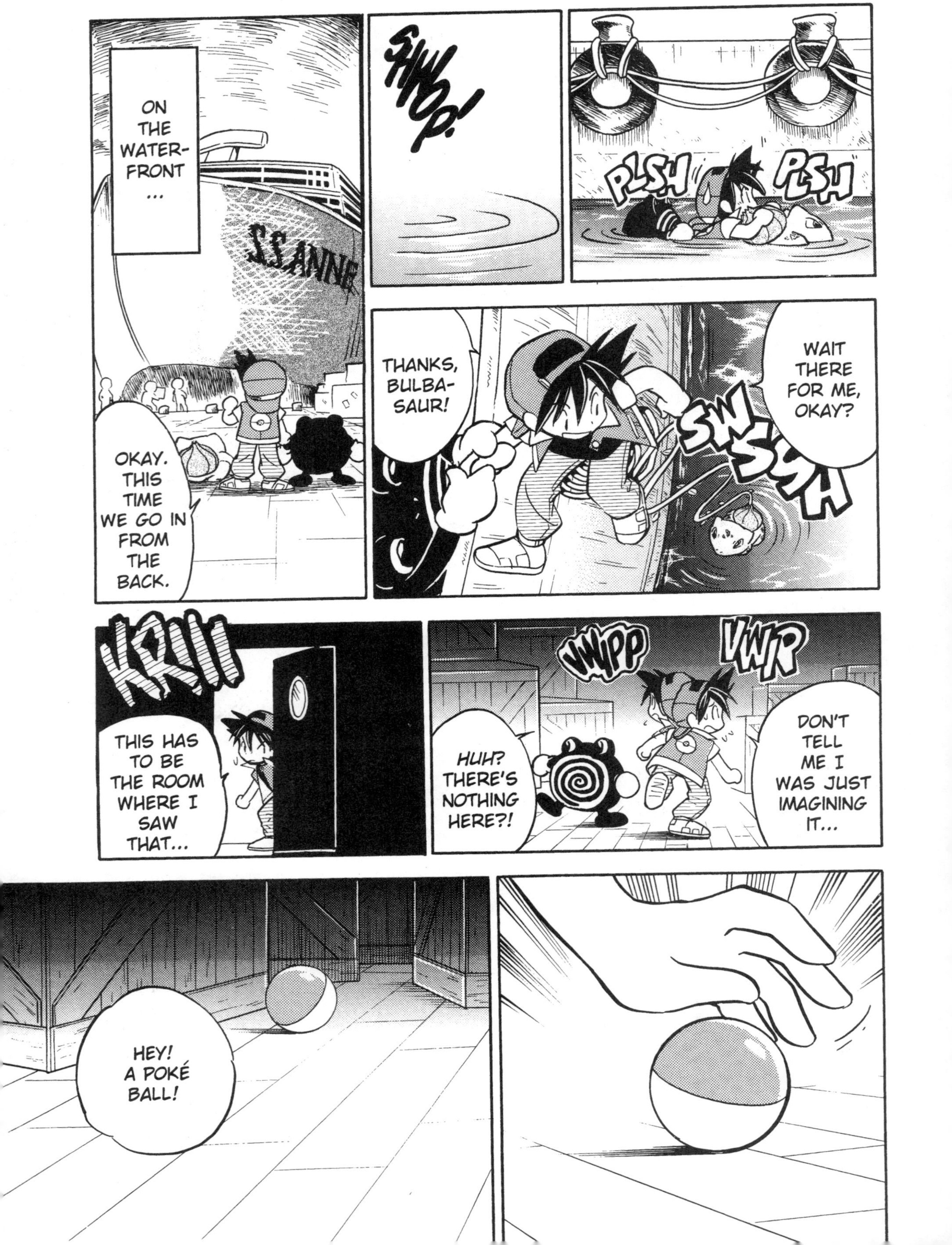
ON THE WATER-FRONT...
S.S. ANNE
SHWOOP!
PLSH
PLSH
OKAY. THIS TIME WE GO IN FROM THE BACK.
THANKS, BULBA-SAUR!
SWSSH
WAIT THERE FOR ME, OKAY?
KRIII
THIS HAS TO BE THE ROOM WHERE I SAW THAT...
VWIPP
VWIR
HUH? THERE'S NOTHING HERE?!
DON'T TELL ME I WAS JUST IMAGINING IT...
HEY! A POKÉ BALL!

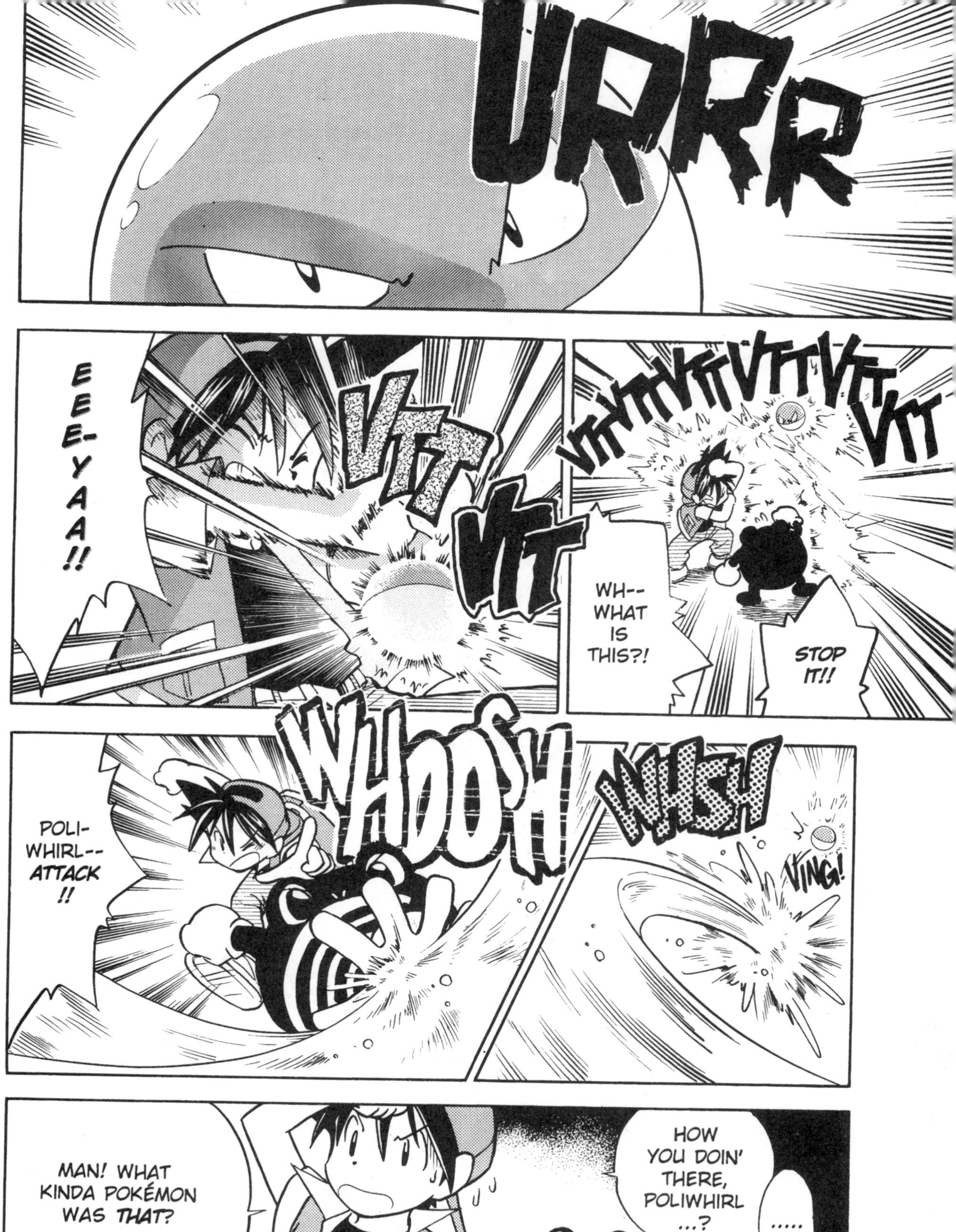
URRR
EEEE-YAAA!!
VTT
VTT
VTTVTTVTTVTTVTTVTT
WH-- WHAT IS THIS?!
STOP IT!!
POLI-WHIRL-- ATTACK!!
WHOOSH
WHSH
VING!
MAN! WHAT KINDA POKÉMON WAS THAT?
HOW YOU DOIN' THERE, POLIWHIRL ...?
.....

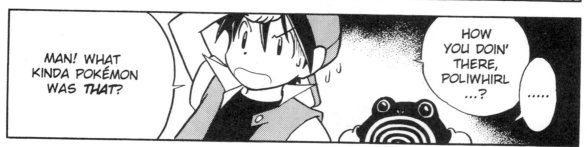

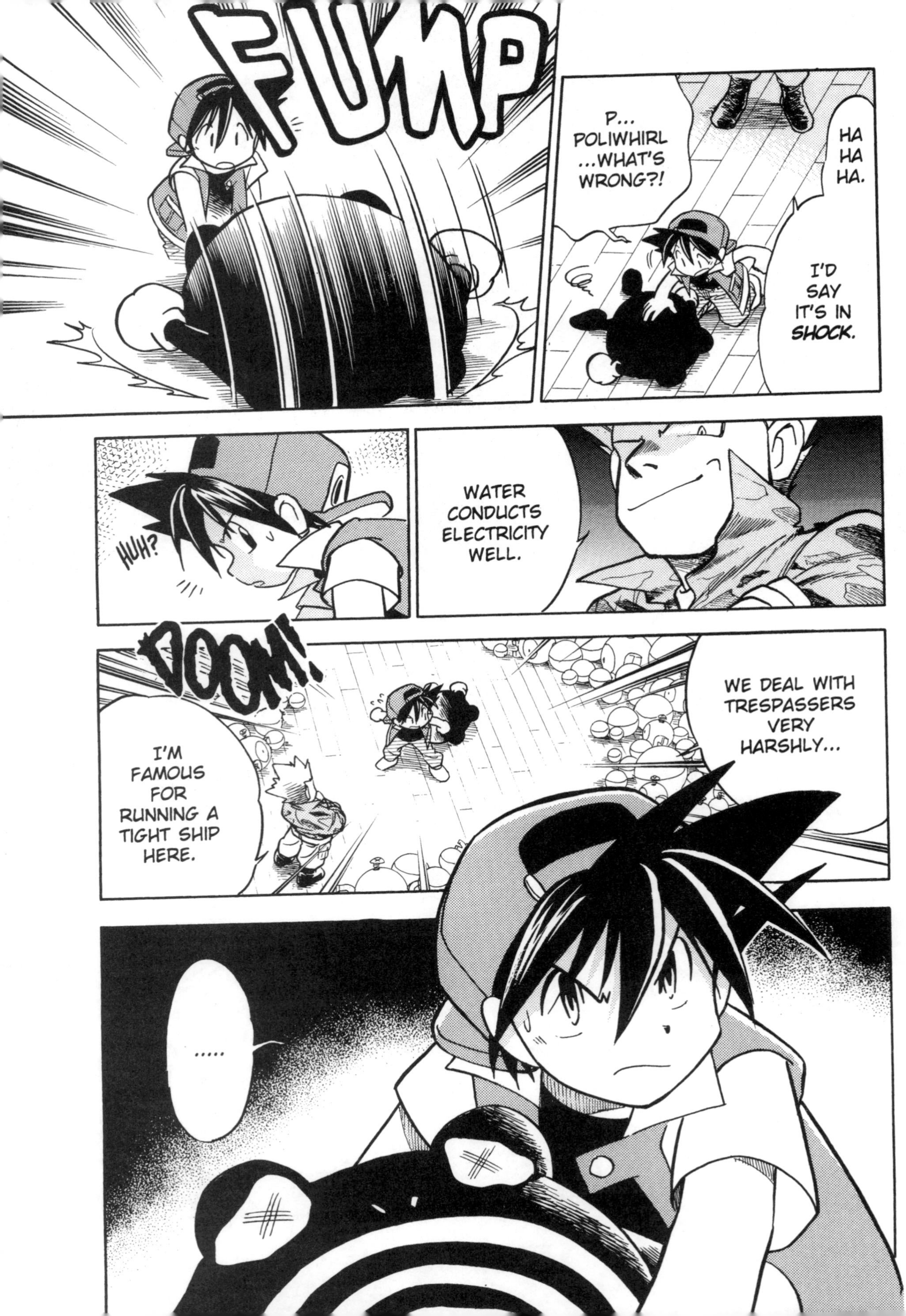
FUMP
P... POLIWHIRL ...WHAT'S WRONG?!
HA HA HA.
I'D SAY IT'S IN SHOCK.
HUH?
WATER CONDUCTS ELECTRICITY WELL.
DOOM!!
I'M FAMOUS FOR RUNNING A TIGHT SHIP HERE.
WE DEAL WITH TRESPASSERS VERY HARSHLY...
.....

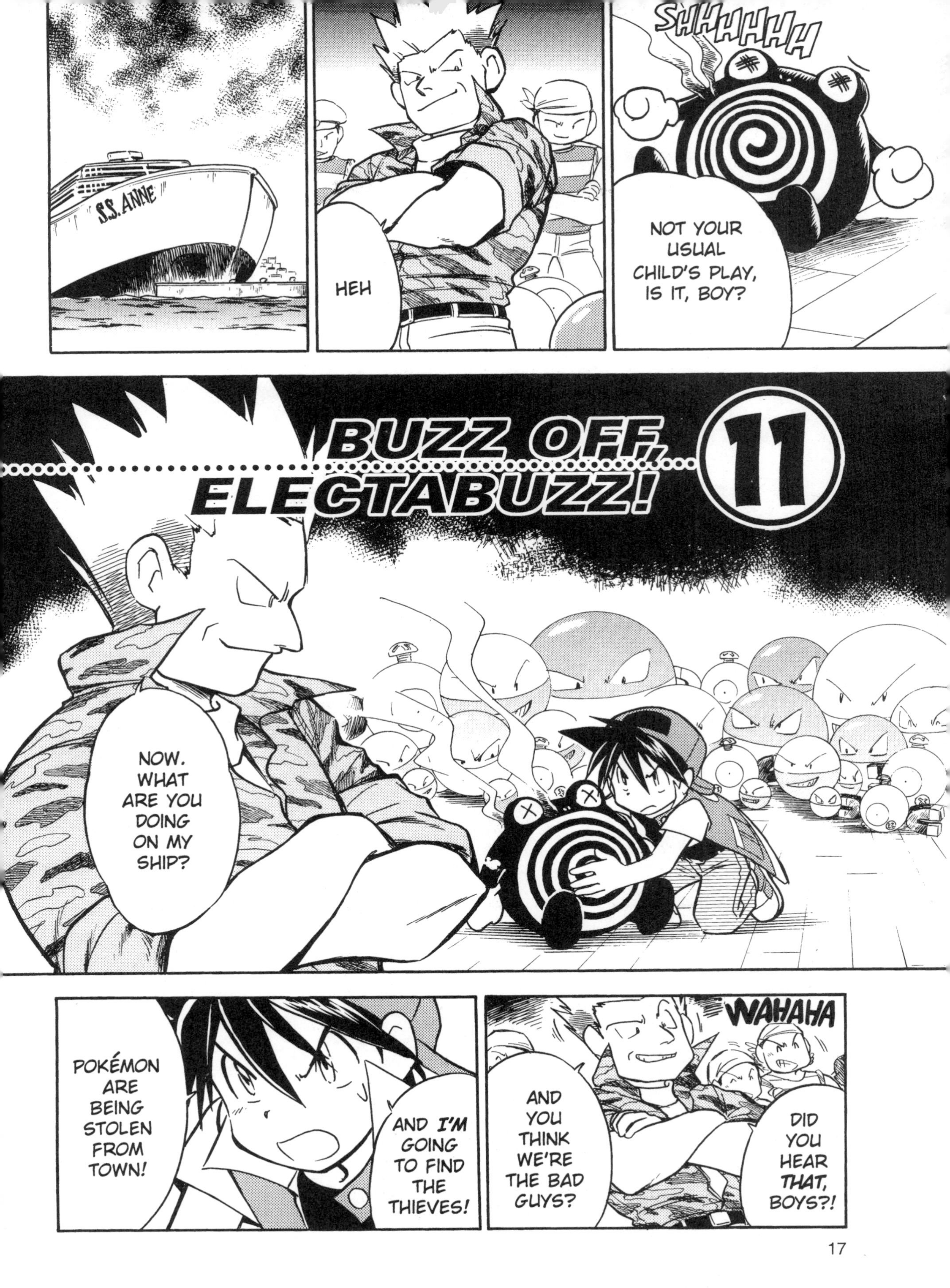
S.S. ANNE
HEH
SHHHHHH
NOT YOUR USUAL CHILD'S PLAY, IS IT, BOY?
BUZZ OFF, ELECTABUZZ!
11
NOW. WHAT ARE YOU DOING ON MY SHIP?
POKÉMON ARE BEING STOLEN FROM TOWN!
AND *I'M* GOING TO FIND THE THIEVES!
WAHAHA
AND YOU THINK WE'RE THE BAD GUYS?
DID YOU HEAR *THAT*, BOYS?!

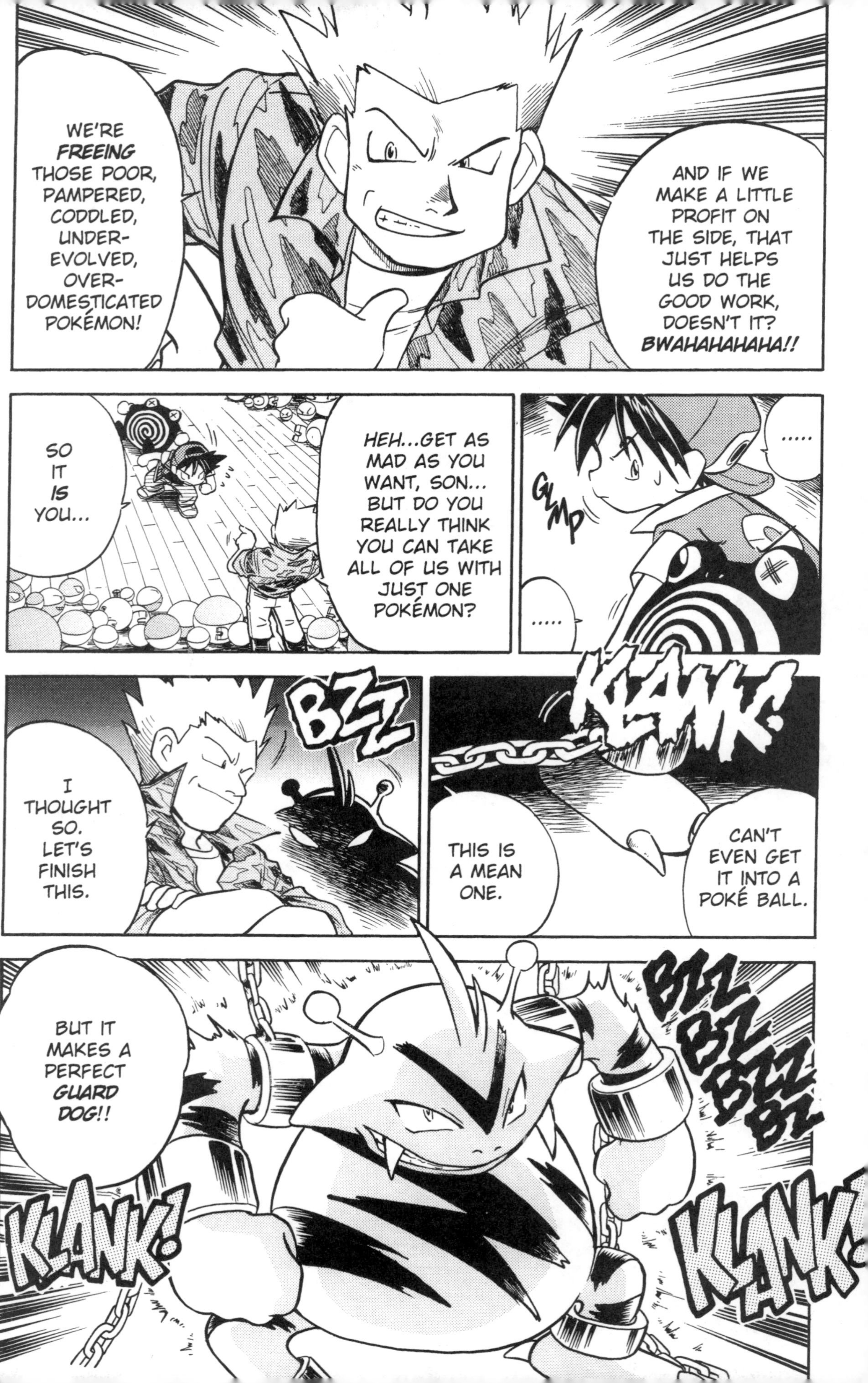

WE'RE FREEING THOSE POOR, PAMPERED, CODDLED, UNDER-EVOLVED, OVER-DOMESTICATED POKÉMON!
AND IF WE MAKE A LITTLE PROFIT ON THE SIDE, THAT JUST HELPS US DO THE GOOD WORK, DOESN'T IT? BWAHAHAHAHA!!
SO IT IS YOU...
HEH...GET AS MAD AS YOU WANT, SON... BUT DO YOU REALLY THINK YOU CAN TAKE ALL OF US WITH JUST ONE POKÉMON?
.....
GLMP
.....
I THOUGHT SO. LET'S FINISH THIS.
BZZ
KLANK!
THIS IS A MEAN ONE.
CAN'T EVEN GET IT INTO A POKÉ BALL.
BUT IT MAKES A PERFECT GUARD DOG!!
BZZ BZ BZZ BZ
KLANK!
KLANK!

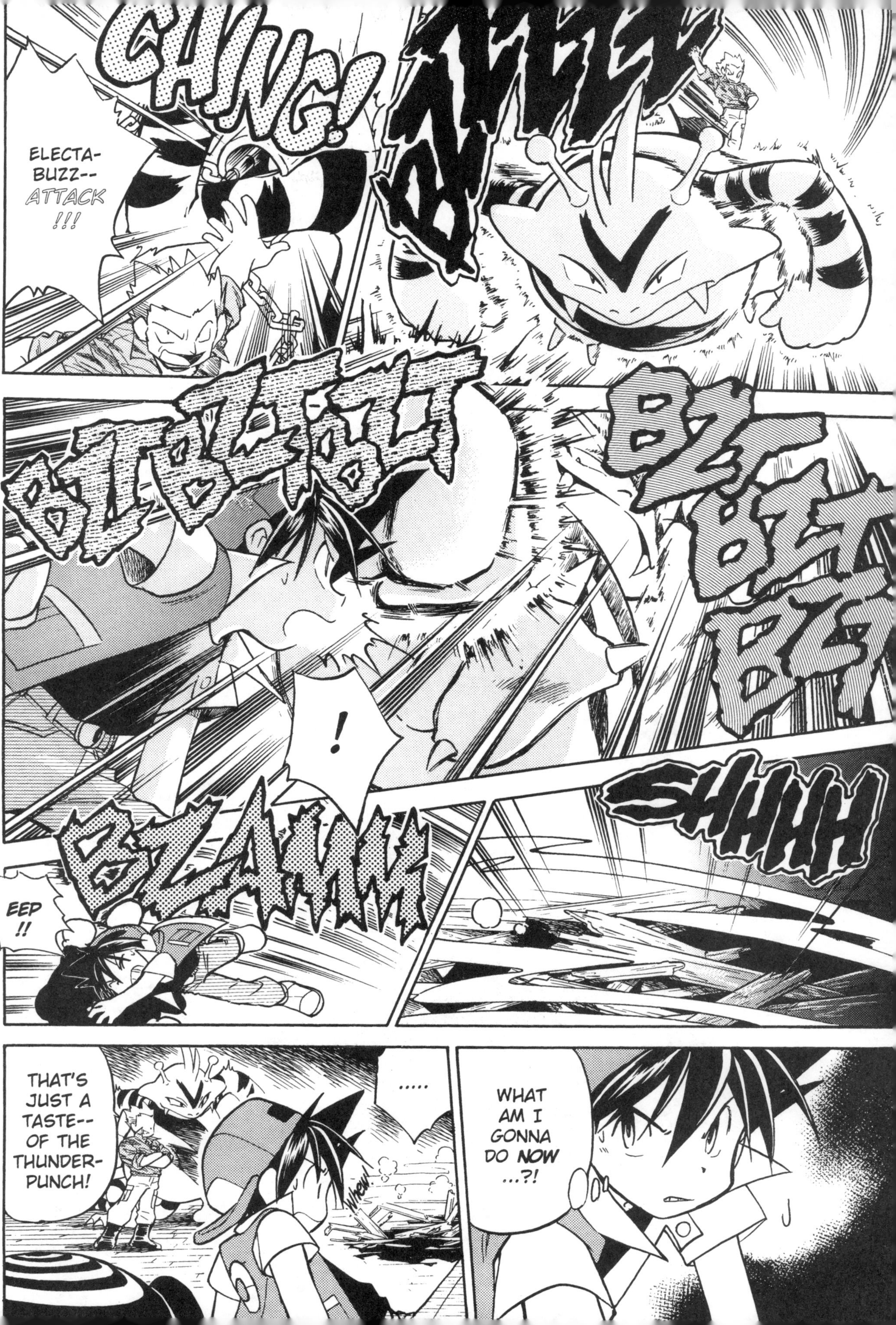
CHING!
ELECTA-BUZZ-- ATTACK!!!
!
EEP!!
THAT'S JUST A TASTE-- OF THE THUNDER-PUNCH!
.....
WHAT AM I GONNA DO NOW ...?!

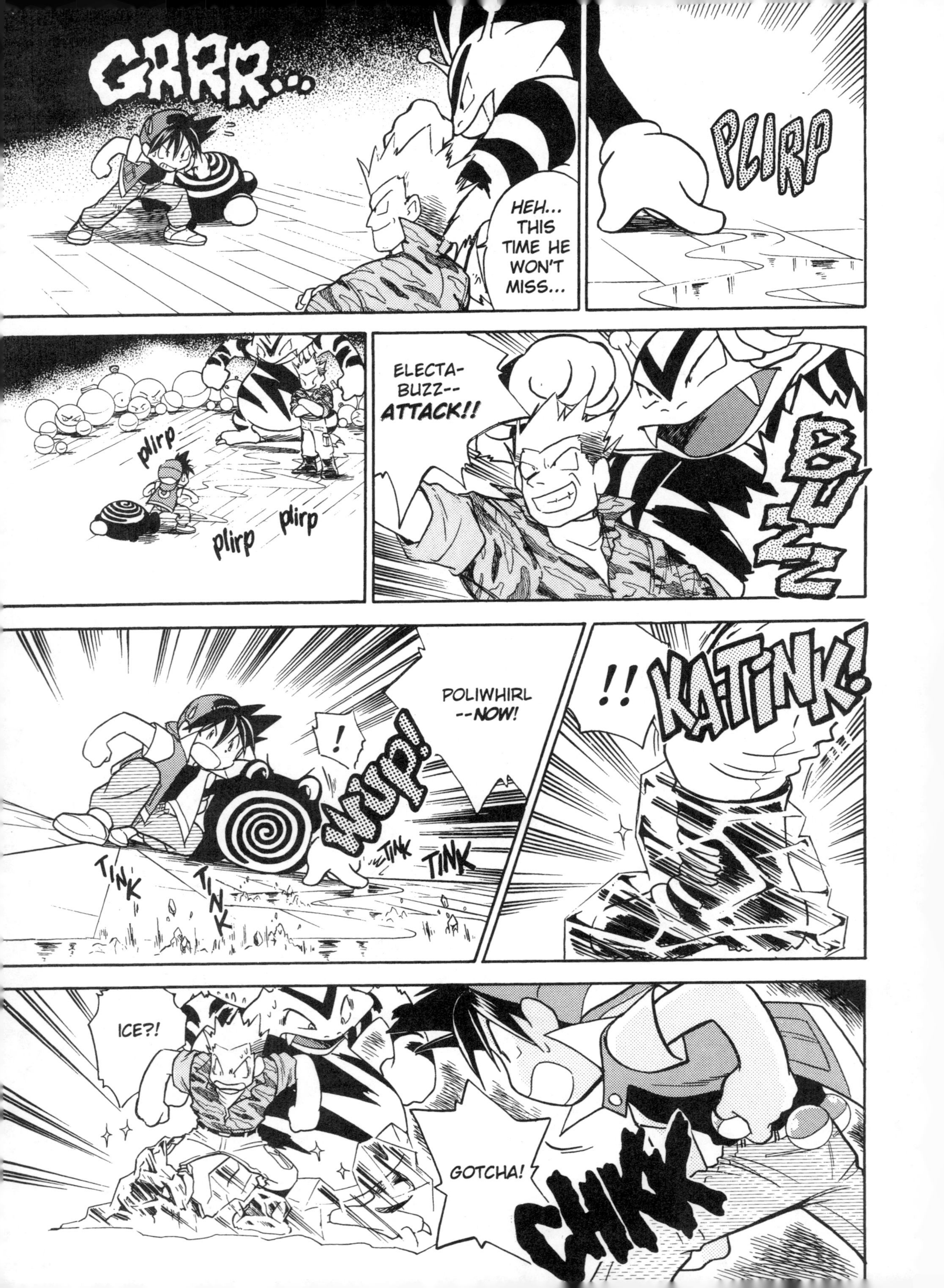
GRRR...
HEH... THIS TIME HE WON'T MISS...
PLIRP
plirp
plirp
plirp
ELECTA-BUZZ--**ATTACK!!**
BUZZ
POLIWHIRL --**NOW!**
!
WUP!
TINK
TINK
TINK
TINK
!!
KA-TINK!
ICE?!
GOTCHA!
CHIK

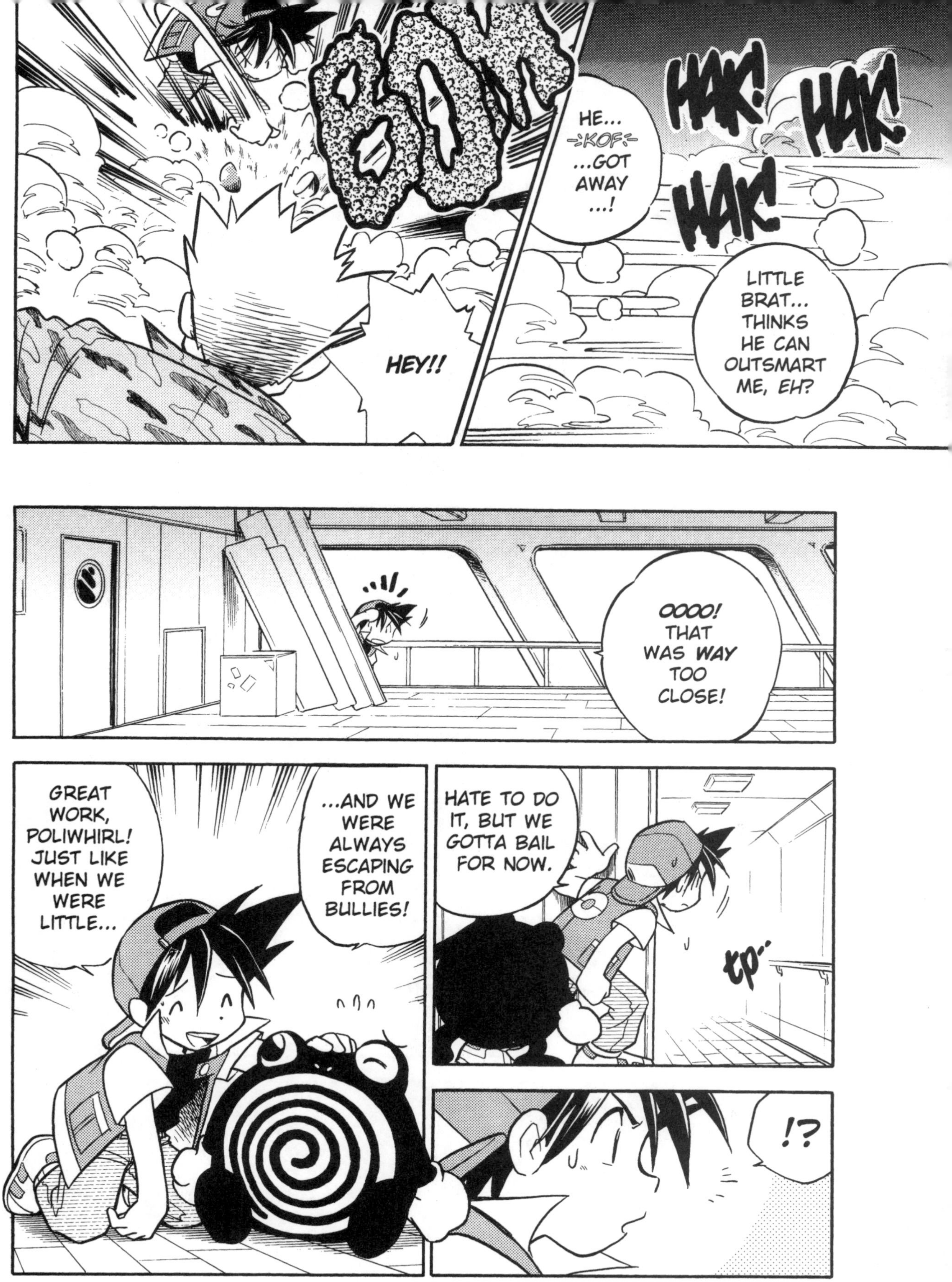
BOOM
HEY!!
HE... -KOF- ...GOT AWAY ...!
HAK! HAK! HAK!
LITTLE BRAT... THINKS HE CAN OUTSMART ME, EH?
OOOO! THAT WAS WAY TOO CLOSE!
GREAT WORK, POLIWHIRL! JUST LIKE WHEN WE WERE LITTLE...
...AND WE WERE ALWAYS ESCAPING FROM BULLIES!
HATE TO DO IT, BUT WE GOTTA BAIL FOR NOW.
tp
!?

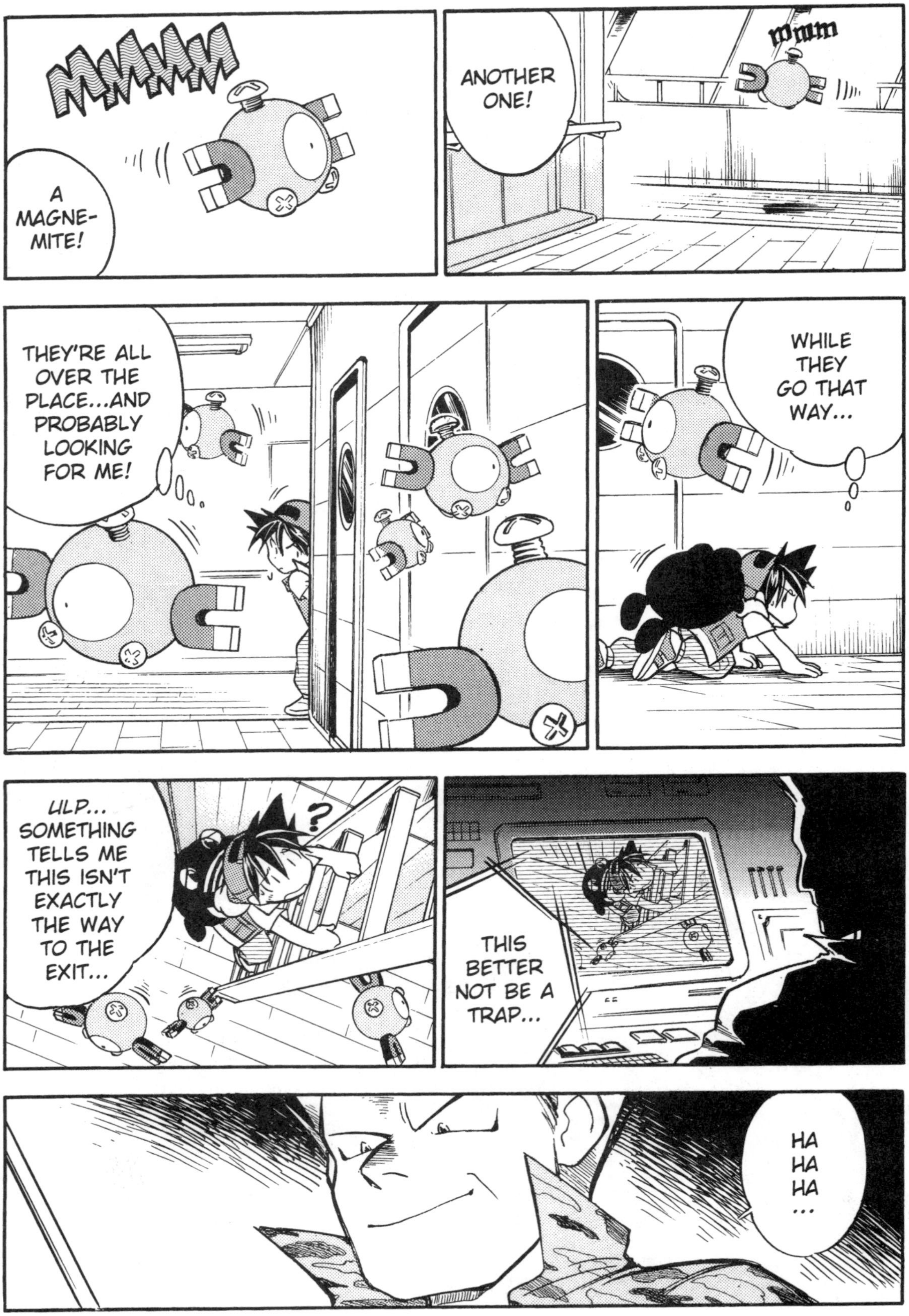
MMMMMMM
A MAGNE-MITE!
ANOTHER ONE!
mmm
THEY'RE ALL OVER THE PLACE...AND PROBABLY LOOKING FOR ME!
WHILE THEY GO THAT WAY...
ULP... SOMETHING TELLS ME THIS ISN'T EXACTLY THE WAY TO THE EXIT...
?
THIS BETTER NOT BE A TRAP...
HA HA HA ...

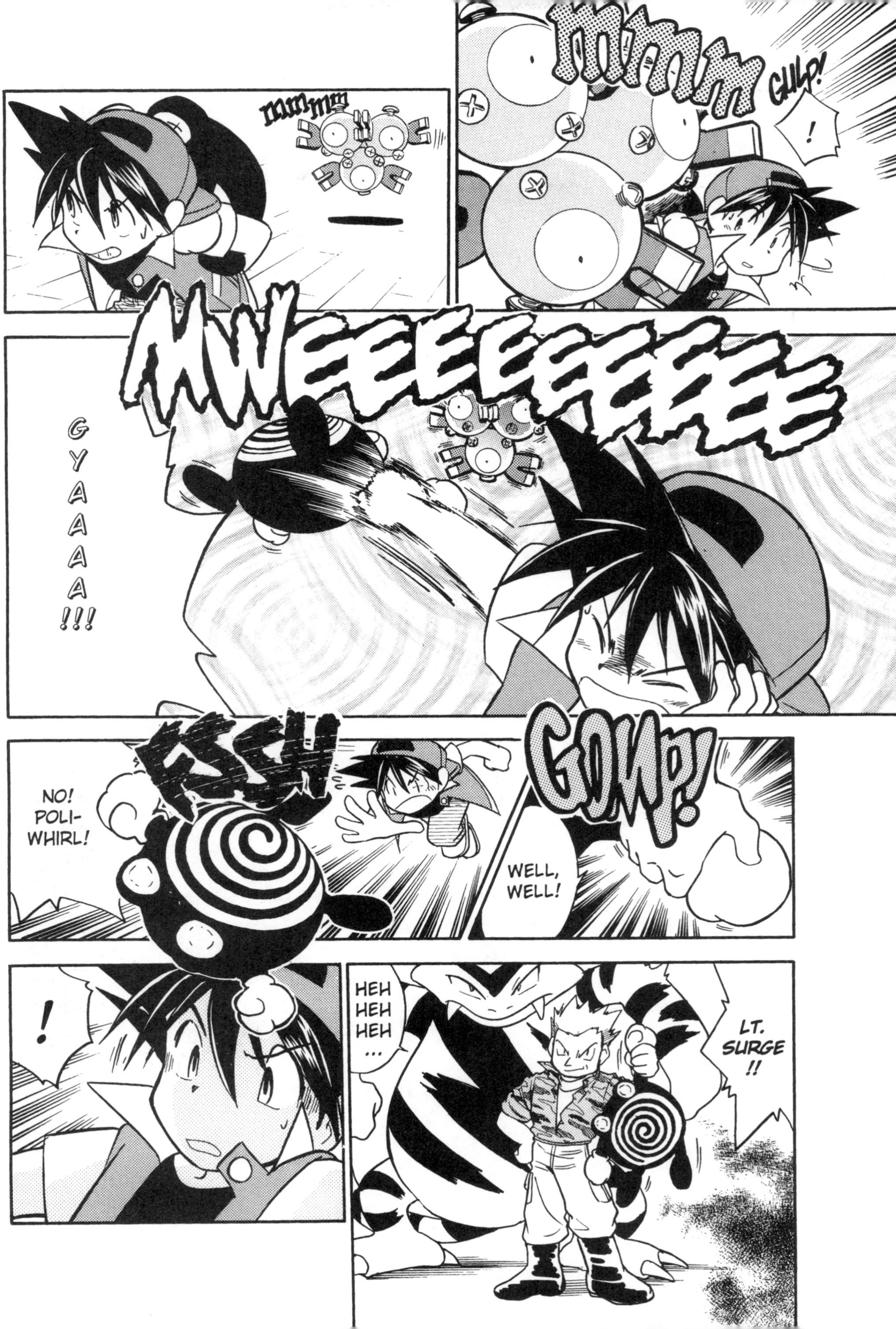
GULP!
!
GYAAAAA!!!
NO! POLI-WHIRL!
WELL, WELL!
!
HEH HEH HEH ...
LT. SURGE !!

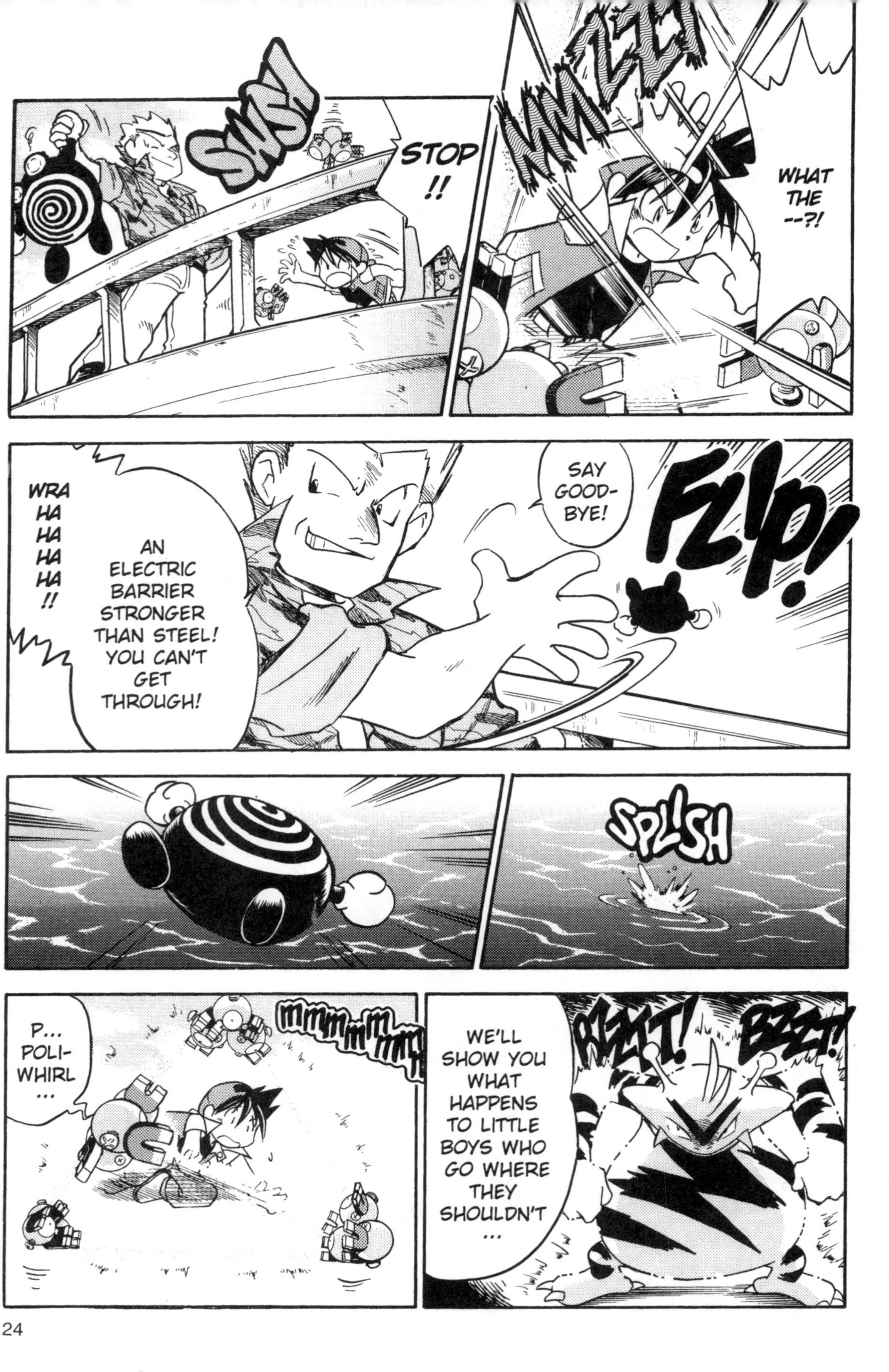
SWSH!
STOP!!
WHAT THE --?!
WRA HA HA HA HA!!
AN ELECTRIC BARRIER STRONGER THAN STEEL! YOU CAN'T GET THROUGH!
SAY GOOD-BYE!
FZIP!
SPLSH
P... POLI-WHIRL...
WE'LL SHOW YOU WHAT HAPPENS TO LITTLE BOYS WHO GO WHERE THEY SHOULDN'T...
BZZT!

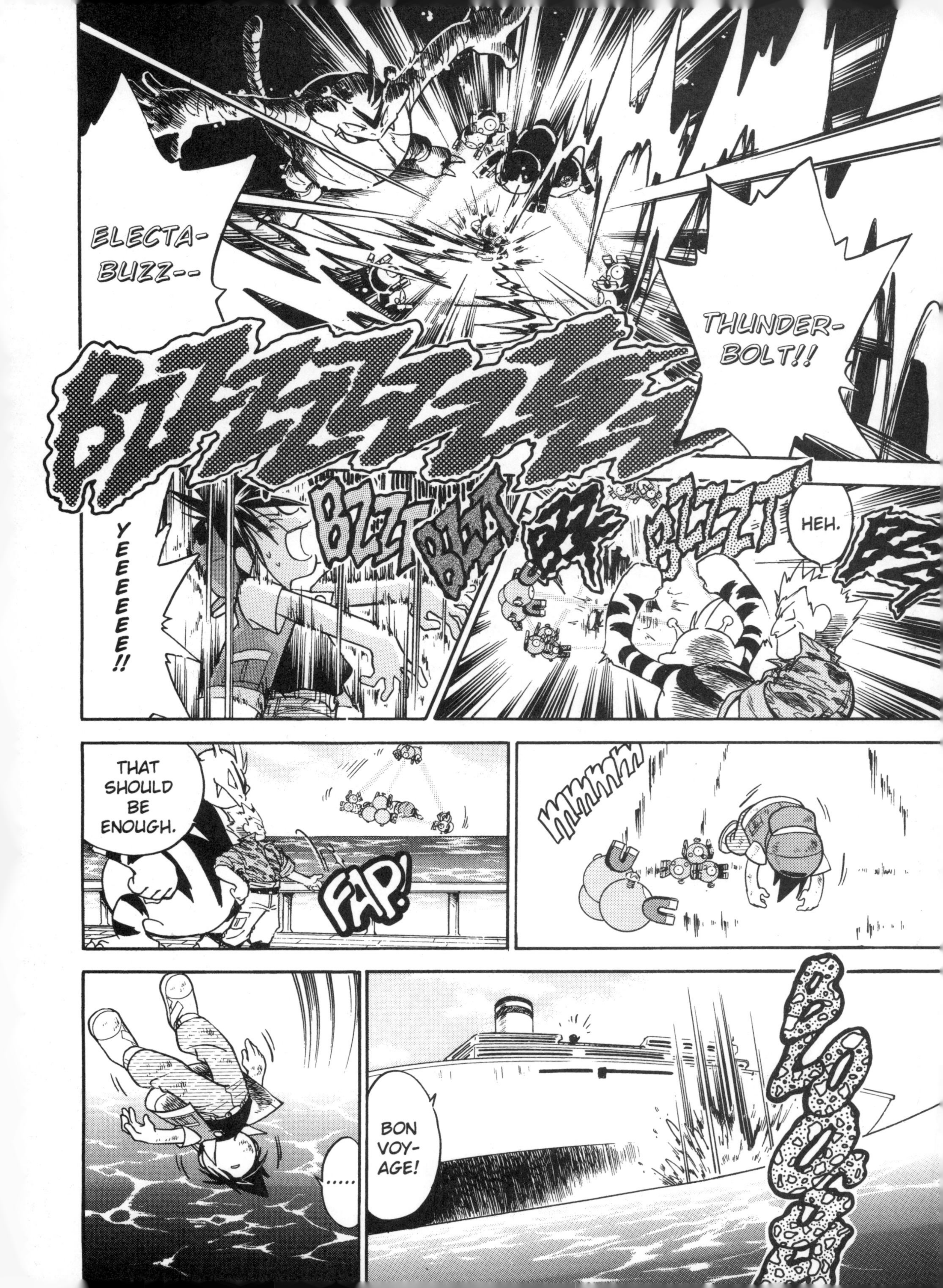
ELECTA-
BUZZ--
THUNDER-
BOLT!!
YEEEEEEEE!!
BZZT
BZZZT
HEH.
THAT
SHOULD
BE
ENOUGH.
FAP!
.....
BON
VOY-
AGE!

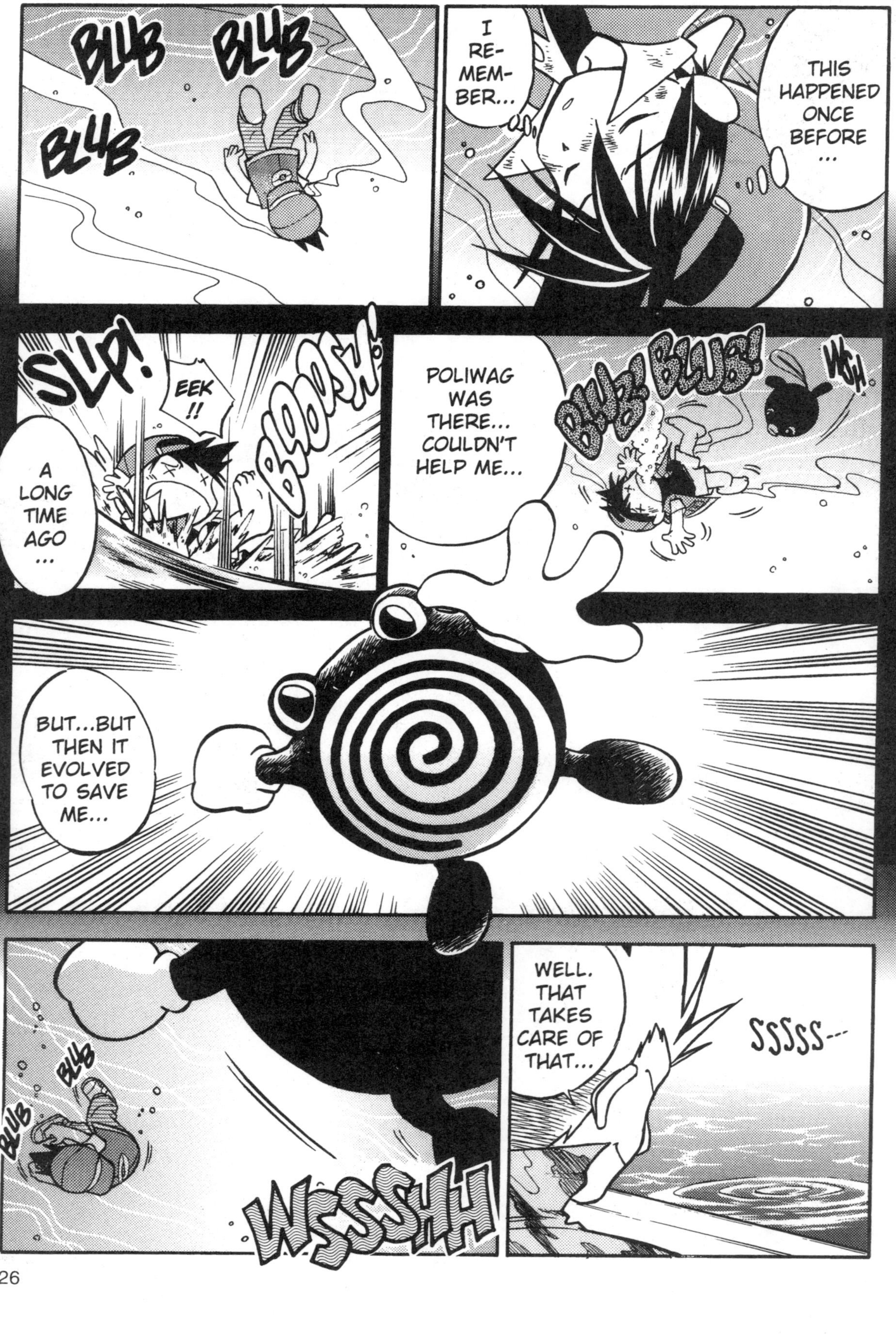
BLUB
BLUB
BLUB
I RE-MEMBER...
THIS HAPPENED ONCE BEFORE ...
SLIP!
EEK !!
BLOOOSH!
A LONG TIME AGO ...
POLIWAG WAS THERE... COULDN'T HELP ME...
BLUB! BLUB!
WSH
BUT...BUT THEN IT EVOLVED TO SAVE ME...
BLUB
BLUB
WSSSHH
WELL. THAT TAKES CARE OF THAT...
SSSSS---

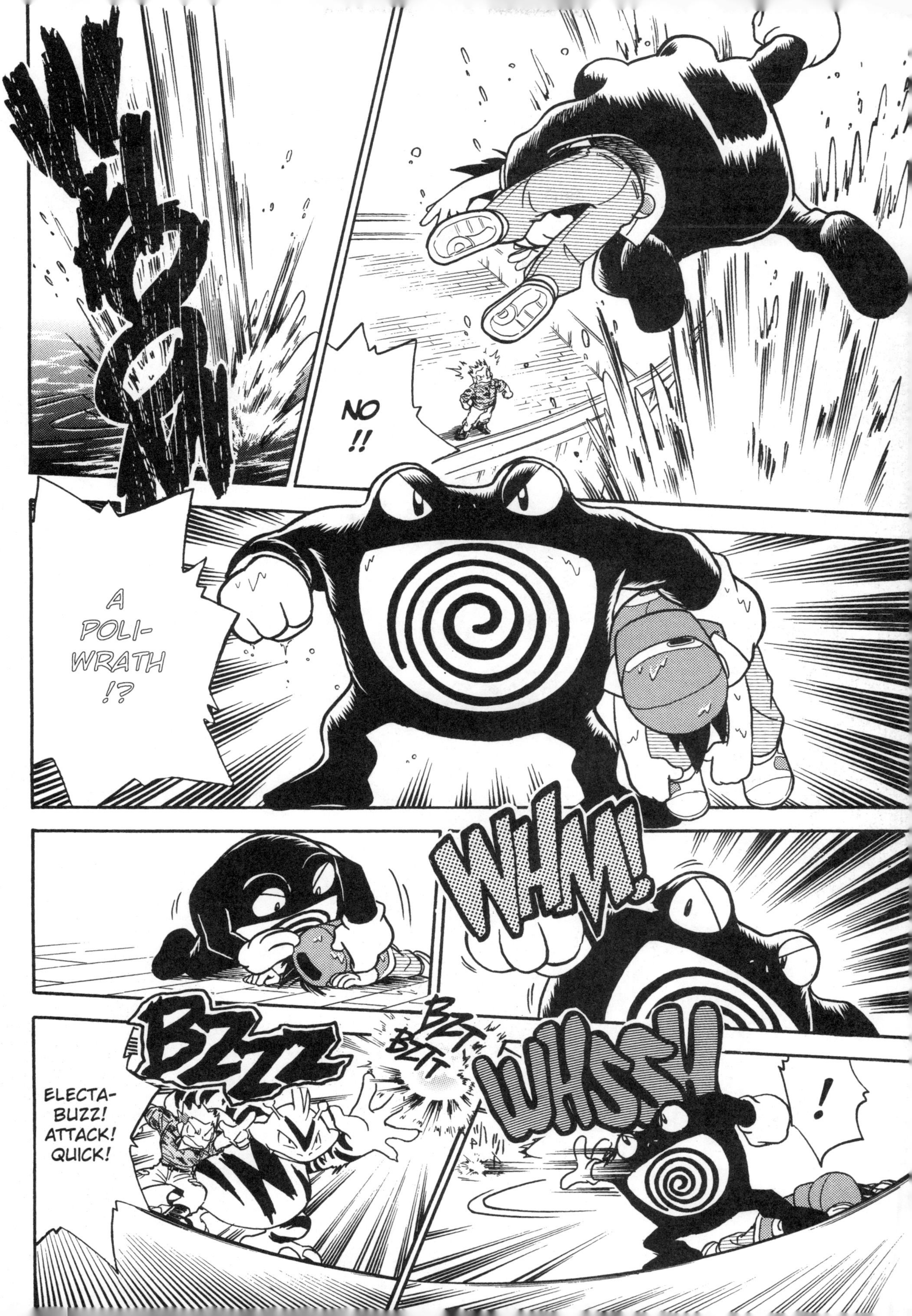

NO !!
A POLI-WRATH !?
WHAM!
ELECTA-BUZZ! ATTACK! QUICK!
BZZZ
BZZT BZZT
WHOOSH!
!

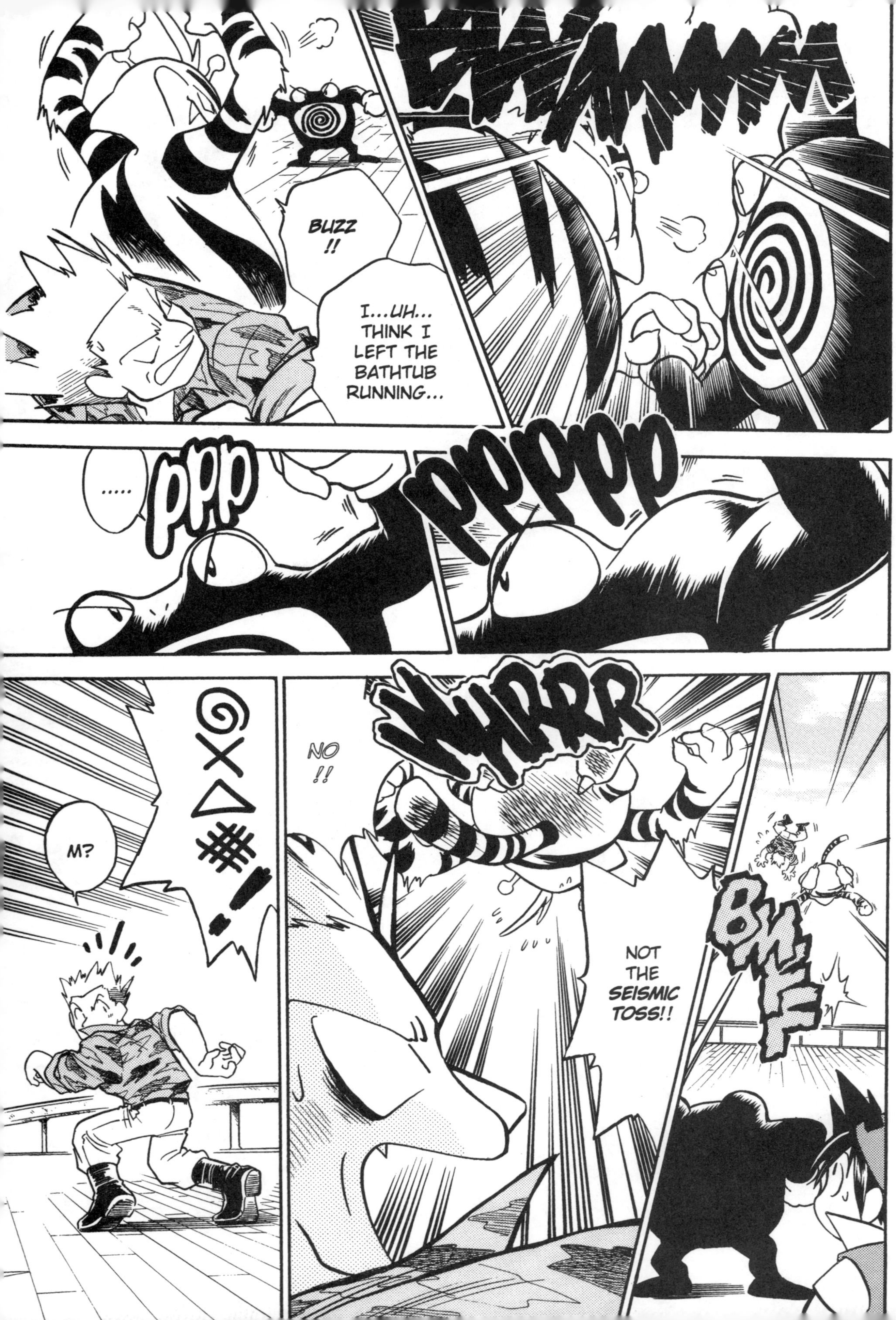
BUZZ !!
I...UH... THINK I LEFT THE BATHTUB RUNNING...
.....
PPP
PPPPPP
M?
NO !!
WHRRR
NOT THE SEISMIC TOSS!!

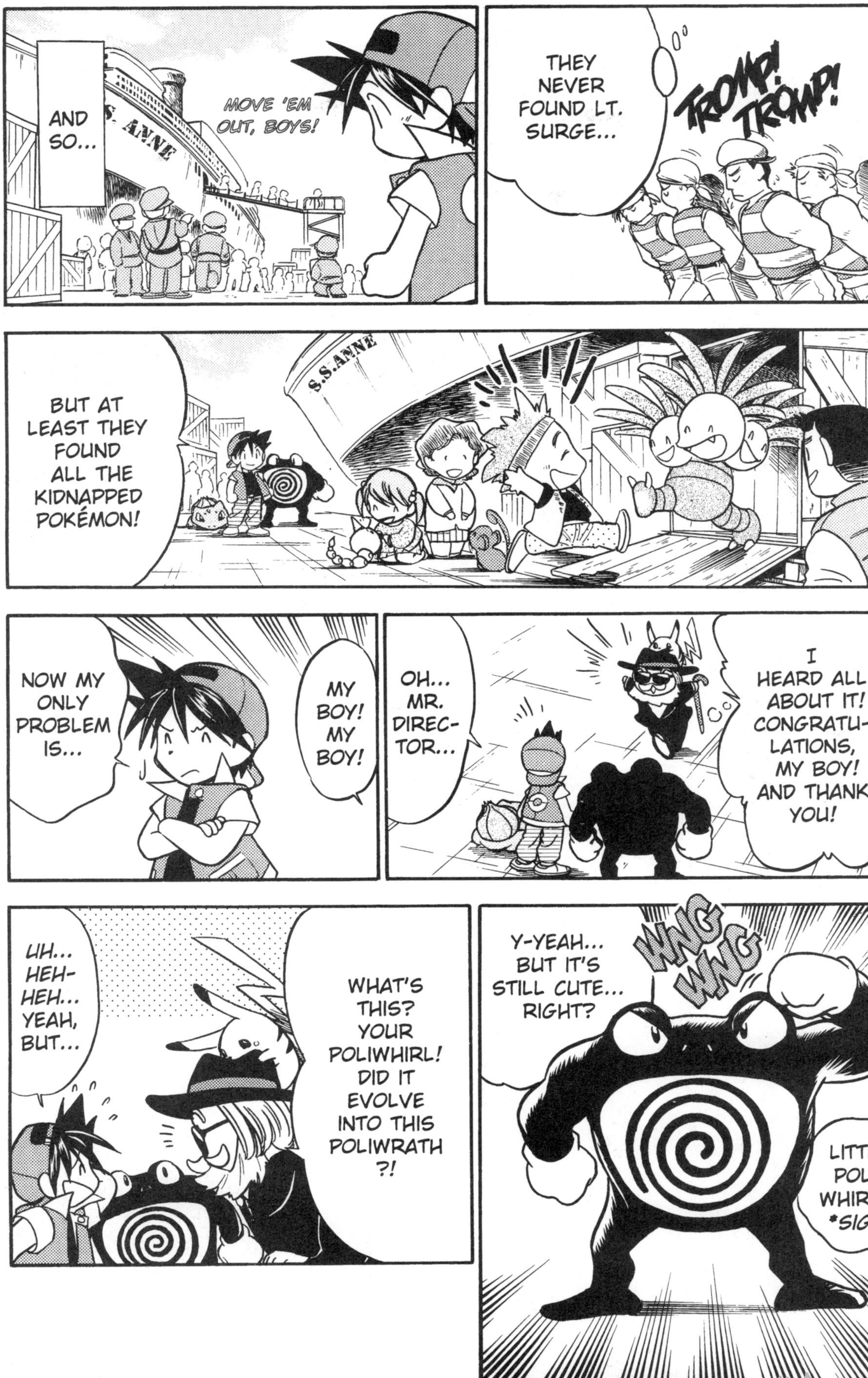
AND SO...
MOVE 'EM OUT, BOYS!
THEY NEVER FOUND LT. SURGE...
TROMP! TROMP!
S.S. ANNE
BUT AT LEAST THEY FOUND ALL THE KIDNAPPED POKÉMON!
S.S. ANNE
NOW MY ONLY PROBLEM IS...
MY BOY! MY BOY!
OH... MR. DIRECTOR...
I HEARD ALL ABOUT IT! CONGRATULATIONS, MY BOY! AND THANK YOU!
UH... HEH-HEH... YEAH, BUT...
WHAT'S THIS? YOUR POLIWHIRL! DID IT EVOLVE INTO THIS POLIWRATH ?!
Y-YEAH... BUT IT'S STILL CUTE... RIGHT?
WNG WNG
LITTLE POLIWHIRL... *SIGH*

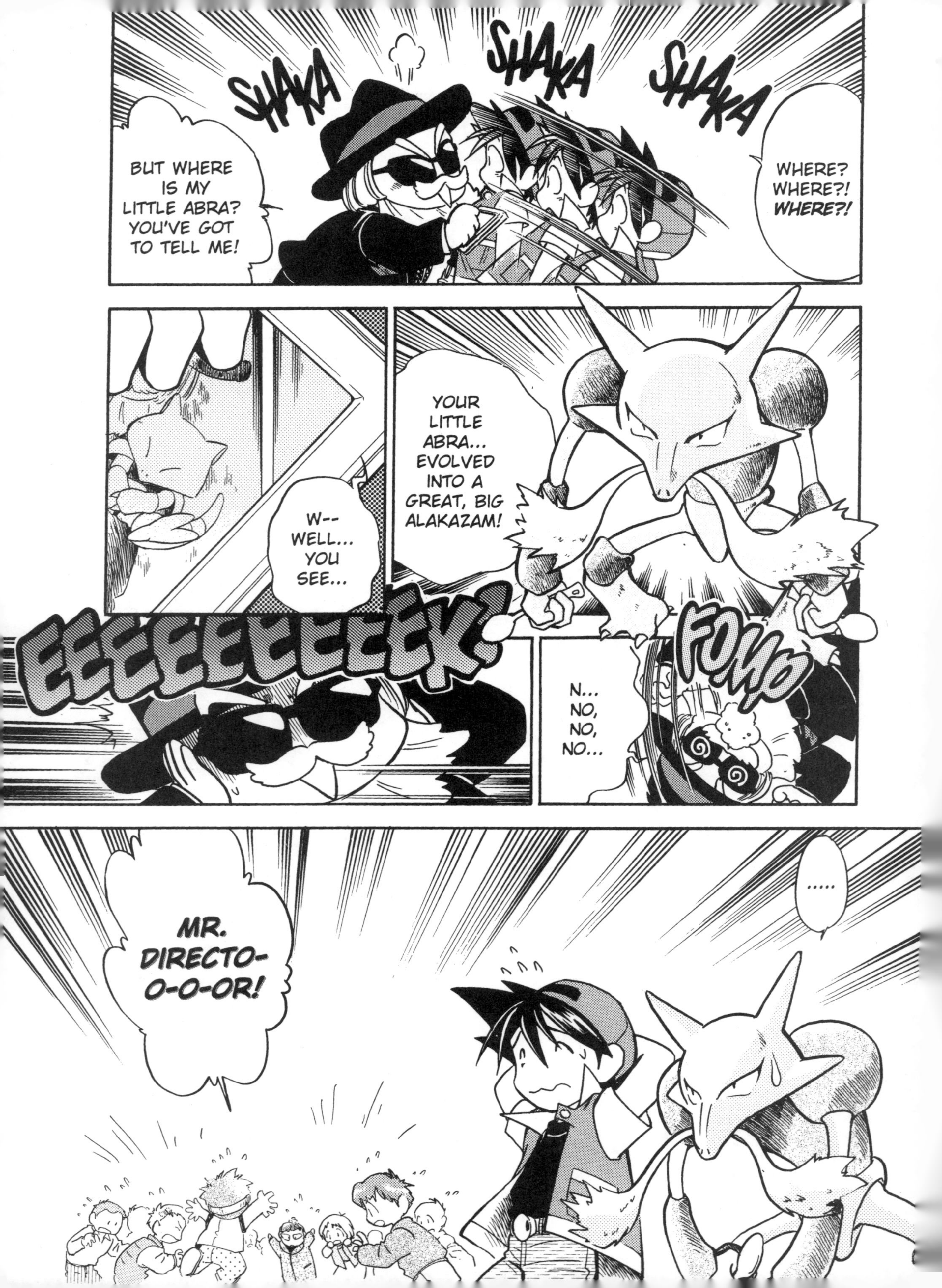
SHAKA SHAKA SHAKA
BUT WHERE IS MY LITTLE ABRA? YOU'VE GOT TO TELL ME!
WHERE? WHERE?! WHERE?!
W-- WELL... YOU SEE...
YOUR LITTLE ABRA... EVOLVED INTO A GREAT, BIG ALAKAZAM!
EEEEEEEEEK!
FOMP
N... NO, NO, NO...
MR. DIRECTO-O-O-OR!
.....

CHAPTER 12

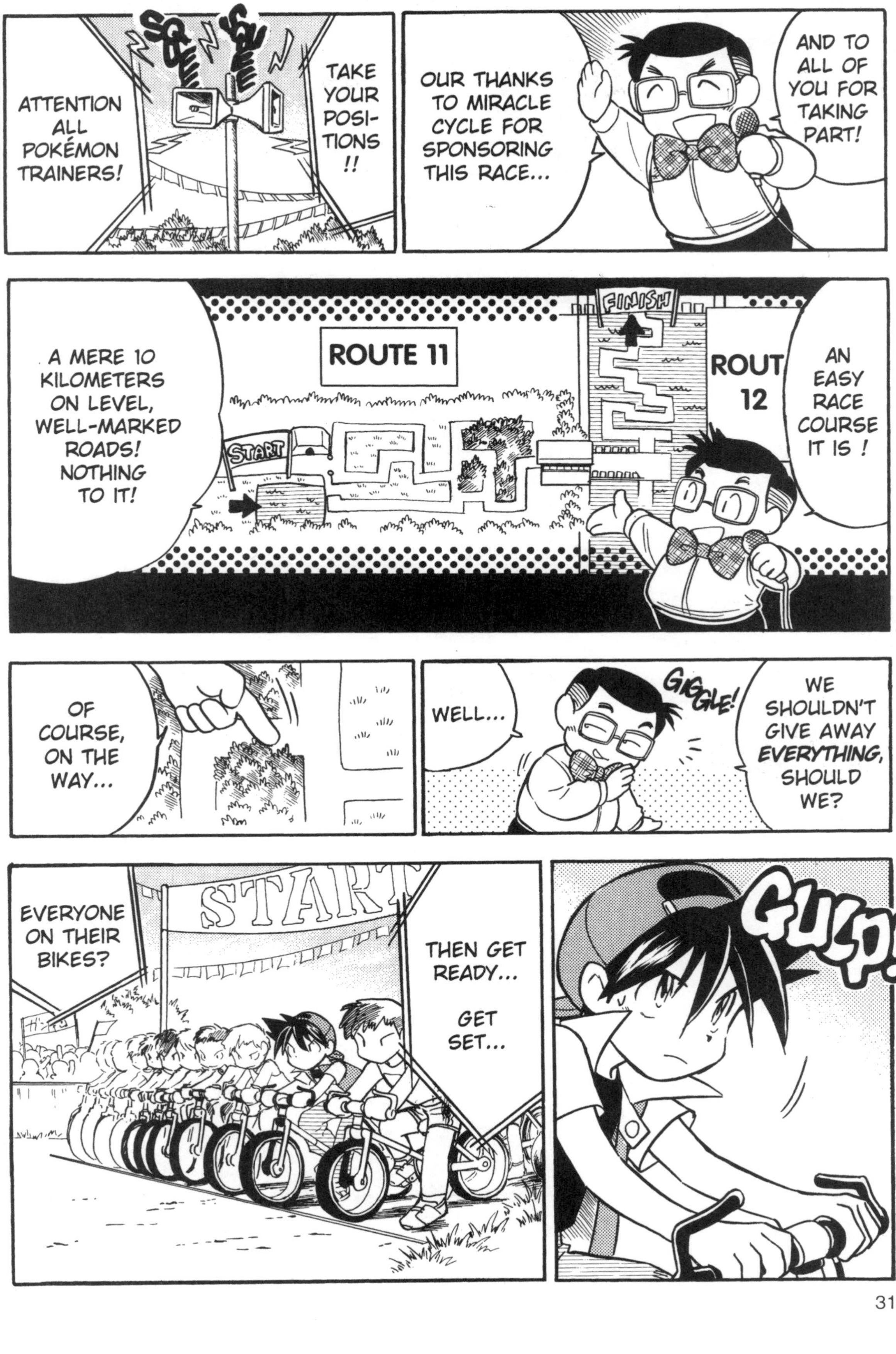

SQUEE
SQUEE
ATTENTION ALL POKÉMON TRAINERS!
TAKE YOUR POSI-TIONS !!
OUR THANKS TO MIRACLE CYCLE FOR SPONSORING THIS RACE...
AND TO ALL OF YOU FOR TAKING PART!
A MERE 10 KILOMETERS ON LEVEL, WELL-MARKED ROADS! NOTHING TO IT!
ROUTE 11
START
FINISH
ROUT
12
AN EASY RACE COURSE IT IS !
OF COURSE, ON THE WAY...
WELL...
GIGGLE!
WE SHOULDN'T GIVE AWAY EVERYTHING, SHOULD WE?
START
EVERYONE ON THEIR BIKES?
THEN GET READY...
GET SET...
GULP!

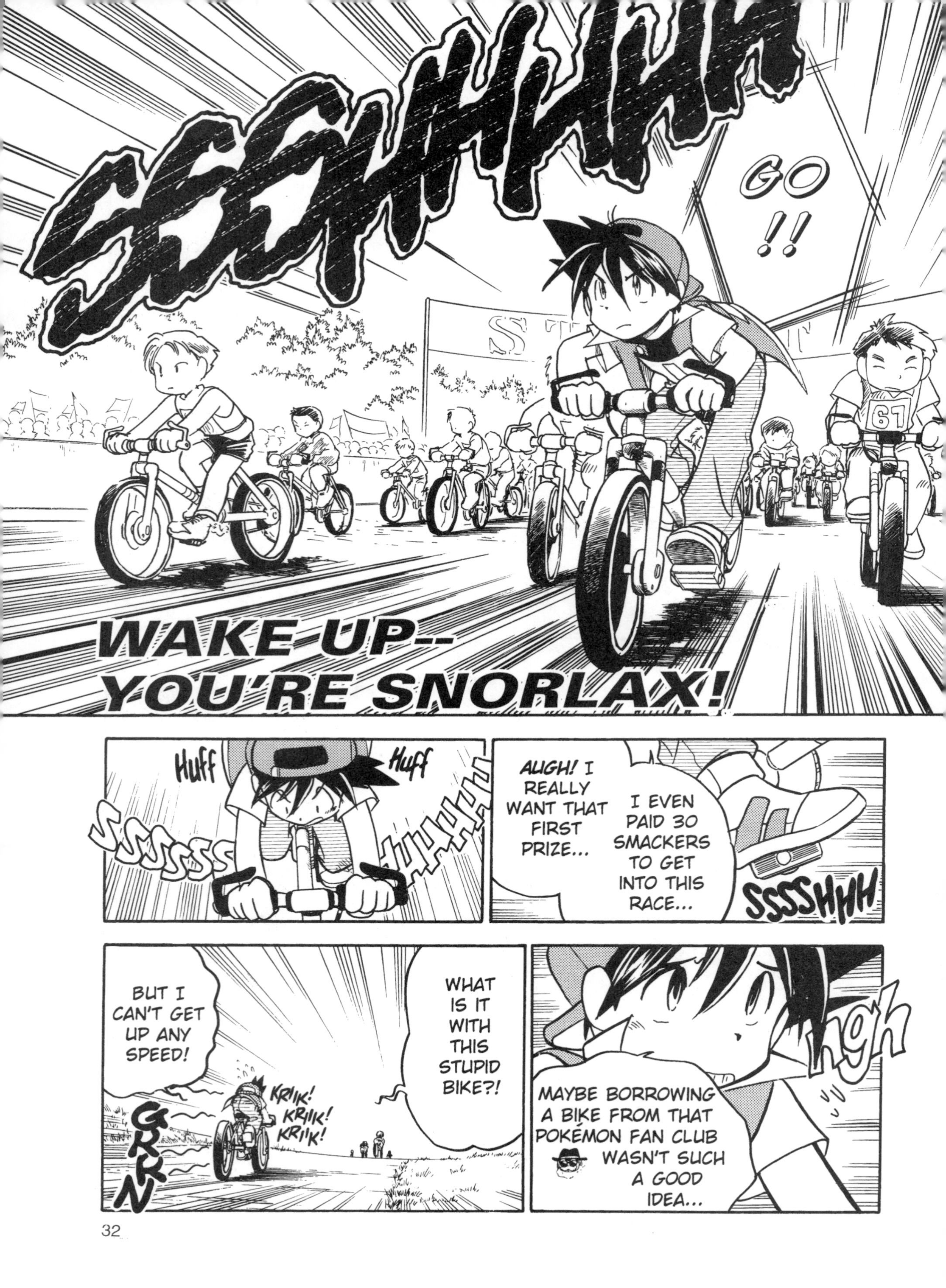
SSSHHHHH
GO !!
WAKE UP-- YOU'RE SNORLAX!
Huff
Huff
SSSSSSHHHHHH
AUGH! I REALLY WANT THAT FIRST PRIZE...
I EVEN PAID 30 SMACKERS TO GET INTO THIS RACE...
SSSSHHH
BUT I CAN'T GET UP ANY SPEED!
WHAT IS IT WITH THIS STUPID BIKE?!
KRIIK! KRIIK! KRIIK!
GRKN
hgh
MAYBE BORROWING A BIKE FROM THAT POKÉMON FAN CLUB WASN'T SUCH A GOOD IDEA...

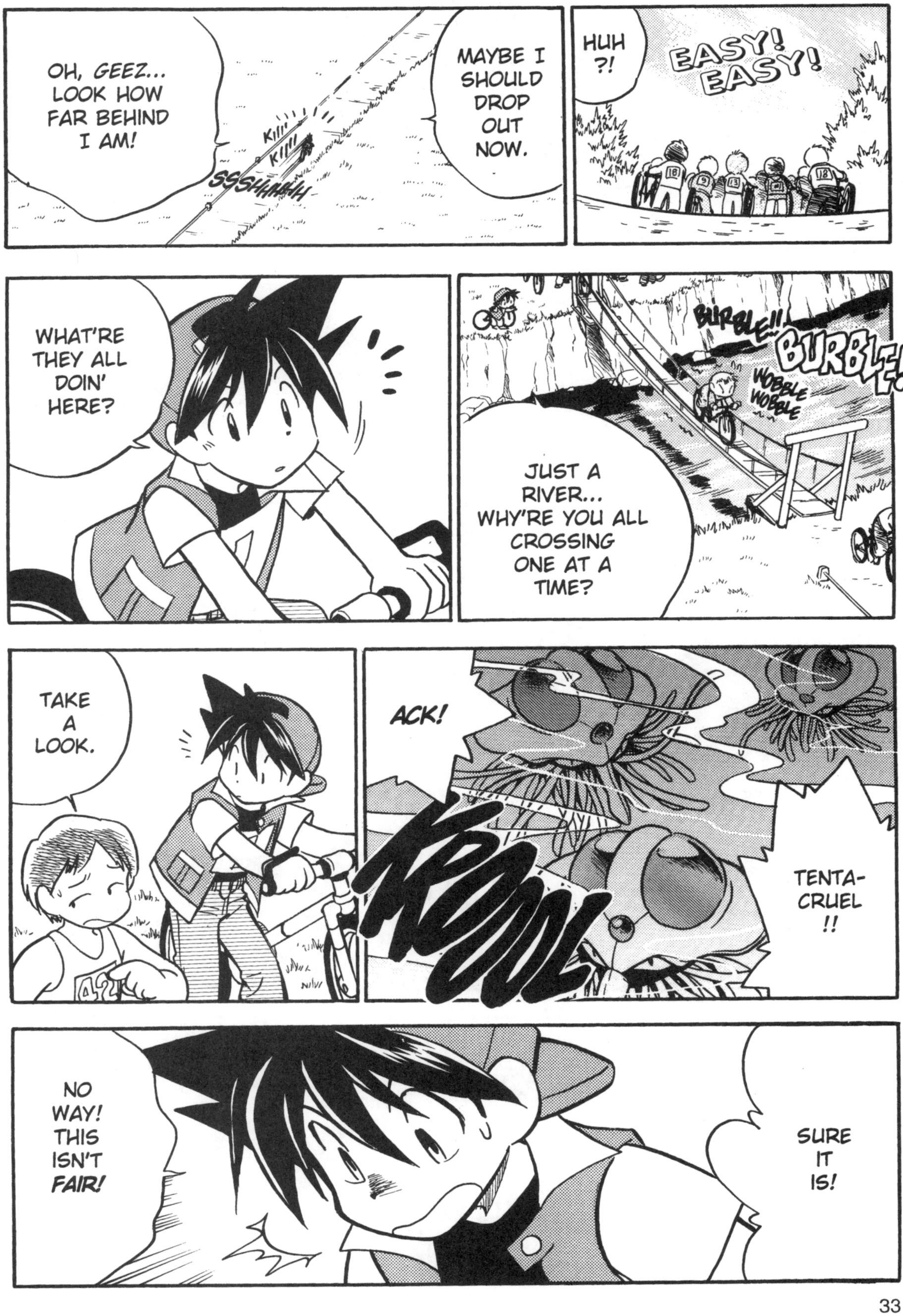

OH, GEEZ... LOOK HOW FAR BEHIND I AM!
KI!!! KI!!!
SSSHHHHH
MAYBE I SHOULD DROP OUT NOW.
HUH ?!
EASY! EASY!
WHAT'RE THEY ALL DOIN' HERE?
BURBLE!! BURBLE!
WOBBLE WOBBLE
JUST A RIVER... WHY'RE YOU ALL CROSSING ONE AT A TIME?
TAKE A LOOK.
ACK!
KROOOL
TENTA-CRUEL !!
NO WAY! THIS ISN'T FAIR!
SURE IT IS!

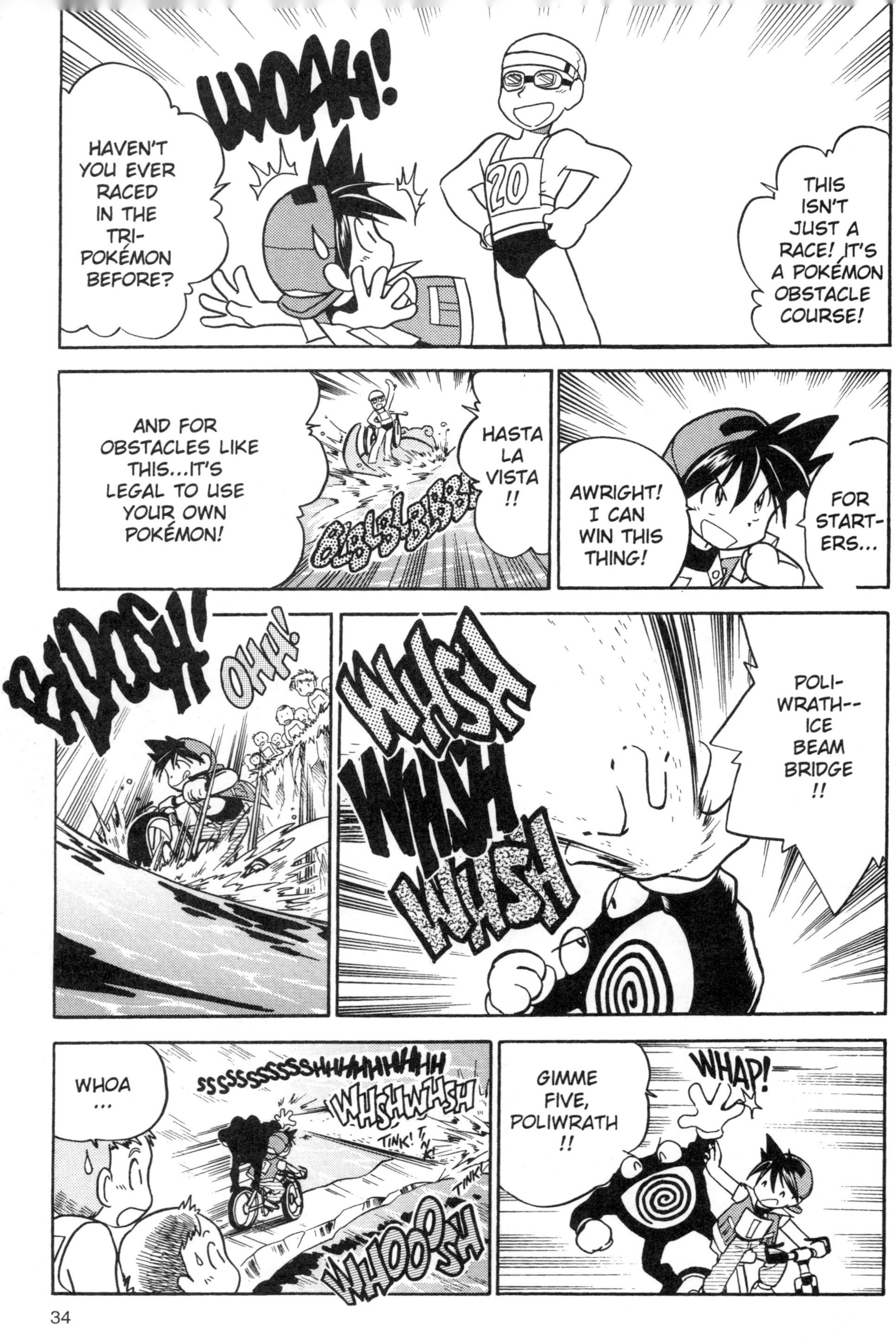
HAVEN'T YOU EVER RACED IN THE TRI-POKÉMON BEFORE?
WOAH!
THIS ISN'T JUST A RACE! IT'S A POKÉMON OBSTACLE COURSE!
AND FOR OBSTACLES LIKE THIS...IT'S LEGAL TO USE YOUR OWN POKÉMON!
HASTA LA VISTA !!
AWRIGHT! I CAN WIN THIS THING!
FOR STARTERS...
BLOOSH!
OHH!
WHSH
WHSH
WHSH
POLI-WRATH-- ICE BEAM BRIDGE !!
WHOA ...
SSSSSSSSSSSHHHHHHHHH
WHSHWHSH
TINK! TINK!
TINK!
WHOOOSH
GIMME FIVE, POLIWRATH !!
WHAP!

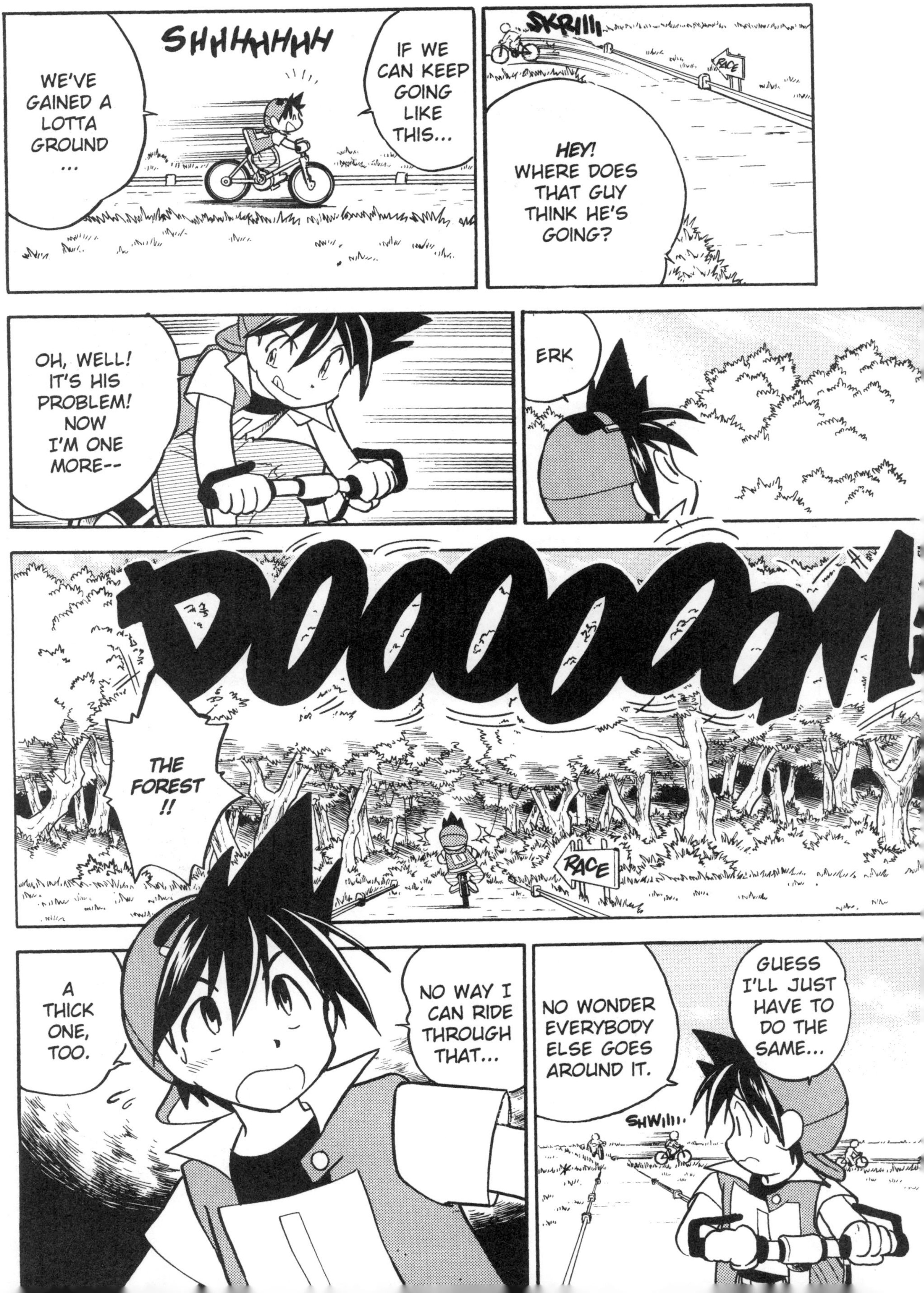
WE'VE GAINED A LOTTA GROUND ...
SHHHHHHH
IF WE CAN KEEP GOING LIKE THIS...
SKRIIII
RACE
HEY! WHERE DOES THAT GUY THINK HE'S GOING?
OH, WELL! IT'S HIS PROBLEM! NOW I'M ONE MORE--
ERK
DOOOOOM
THE FOREST !!
RACE
A THICK ONE, TOO.
NO WAY I CAN RIDE THROUGH THAT...
NO WONDER EVERYBODY ELSE GOES AROUND IT.
GUESS I'LL JUST HAVE TO DO THE SAME...
SHWIIII

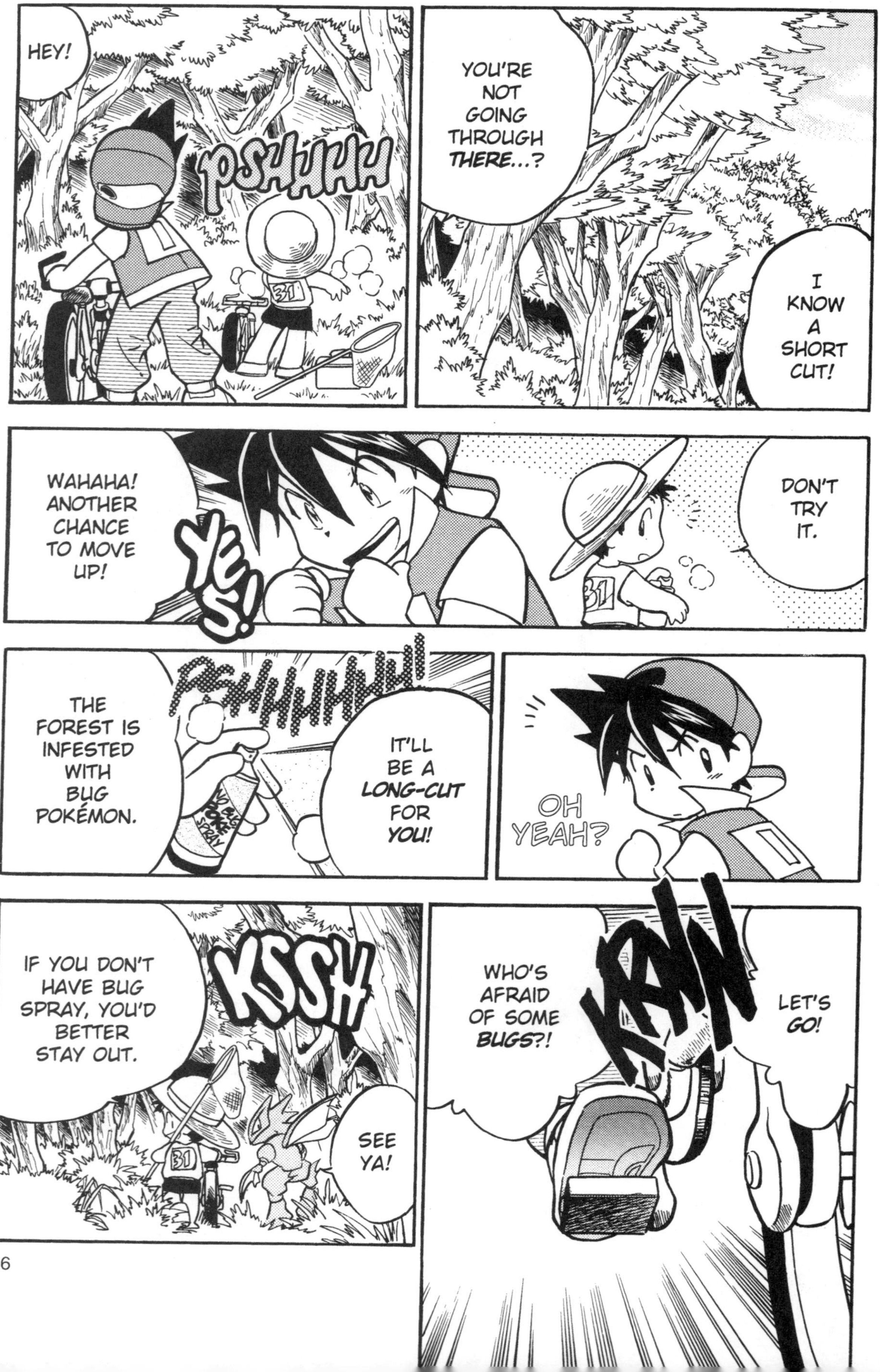
HEY!
PSHHHH
YOU'RE NOT GOING THROUGH THERE...?
I KNOW A SHORT CUT!
WAHAHA! ANOTHER CHANCE TO MOVE UP!
YES!
DON'T TRY IT.
THE FOREST IS INFESTED WITH BUG POKÉMON.
NO BUG POKE SPRAY
IT'LL BE A LONG-CUT FOR YOU!
OH YEAH?
IF YOU DON'T HAVE BUG SPRAY, YOU'D BETTER STAY OUT.
KSSH
SEE YA!
WHO'S AFRAID OF SOME BUGS?!
LET'S GO!

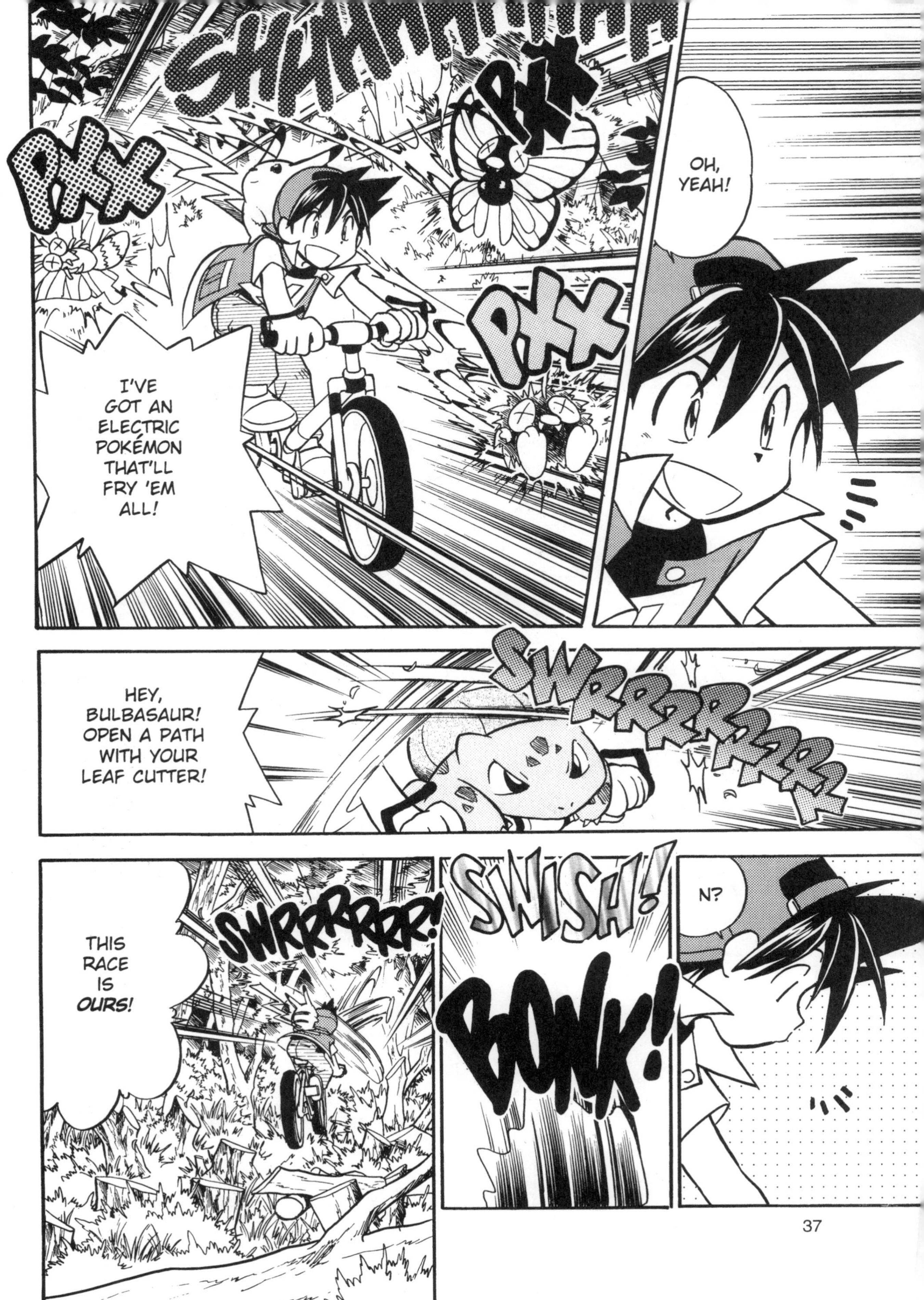
PXX
PXX
PXX
I'VE GOT AN ELECTRIC POKÉMON THAT'LL FRY 'EM ALL!
OH, YEAH!
HEY, BULBASAUR! OPEN A PATH WITH YOUR LEAF CUTTER!
THIS RACE IS *OURS!*
SWISH!
BONK!
N?

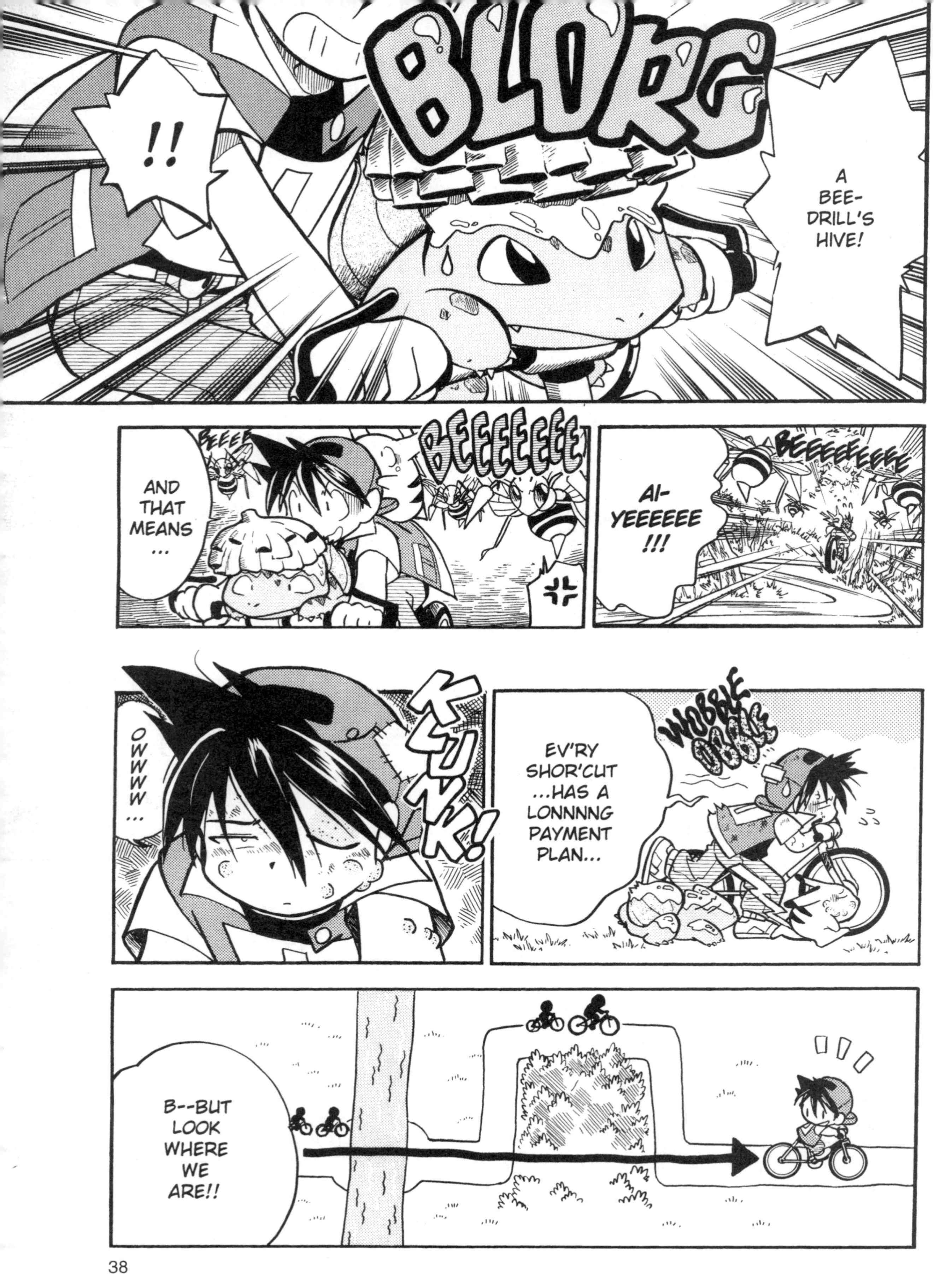

BLORG
!!
A BEE-DRILL'S HIVE!
AND THAT MEANS ...
BEEEEEEE
AI-YEEEEEE !!!
OWWWW...
KLUNK!
WOBBLE
EV'RY SHOR'CUT ...HAS A LONNNNG PAYMENT PLAN...
B--BUT LOOK WHERE WE ARE!!

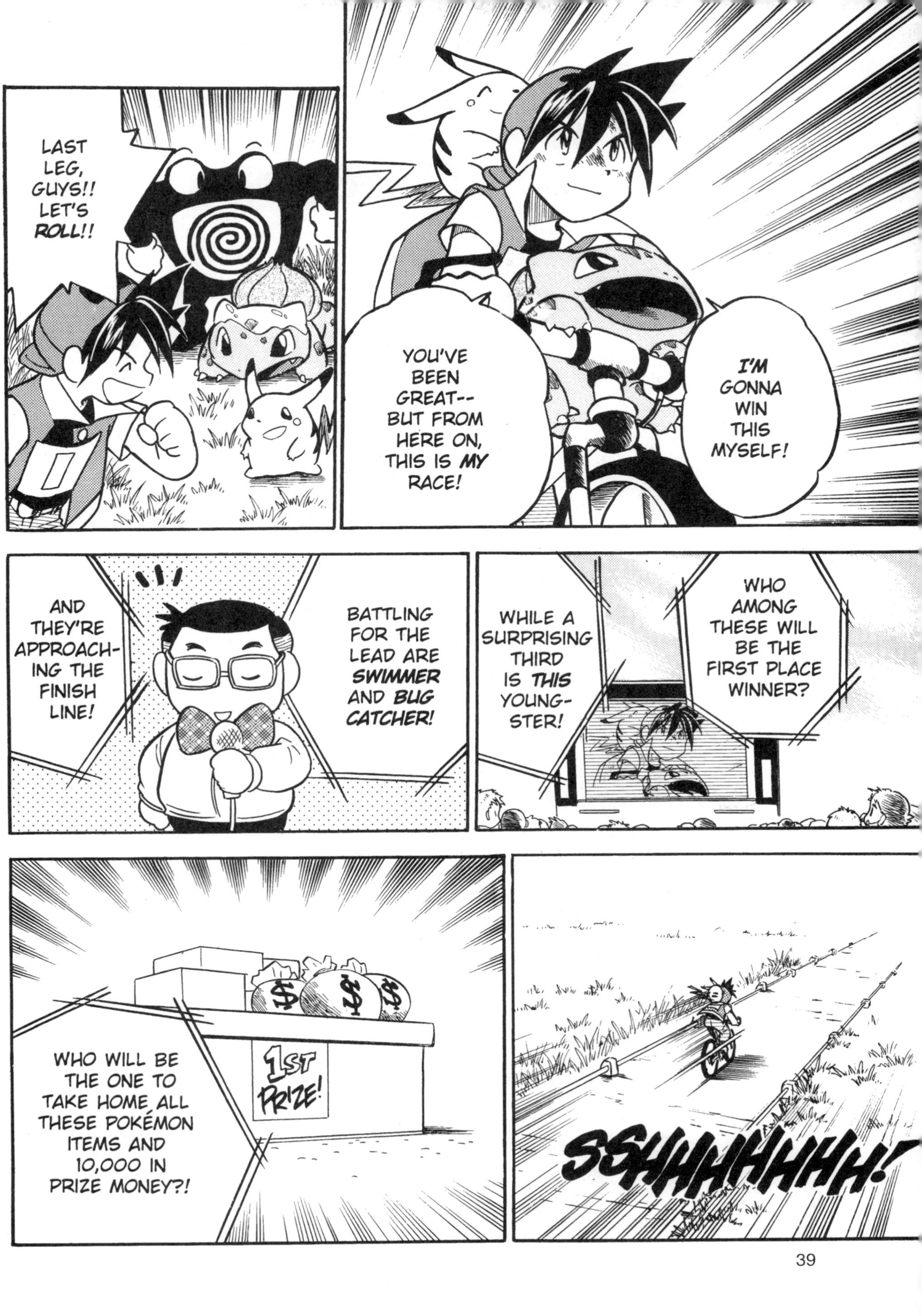

LAST LEG, GUYS!! LET'S ROLL!!
YOU'VE BEEN GREAT-- BUT FROM HERE ON, THIS IS MY RACE!
I'M GONNA WIN THIS MYSELF!
AND THEY'RE APPROACH-ING THE FINISH LINE!
BATTLING FOR THE LEAD ARE SWIMMER AND BUG CATCHER!
WHILE A SURPRISING THIRD IS THIS YOUNG-STER!
WHO AMONG THESE WILL BE THE FIRST PLACE WINNER?
WHO WILL BE THE ONE TO TAKE HOME ALL THESE POKÉMON ITEMS AND 10,000 IN PRIZE MONEY?!
1ST PRIZE!
SSHHHHHHH!

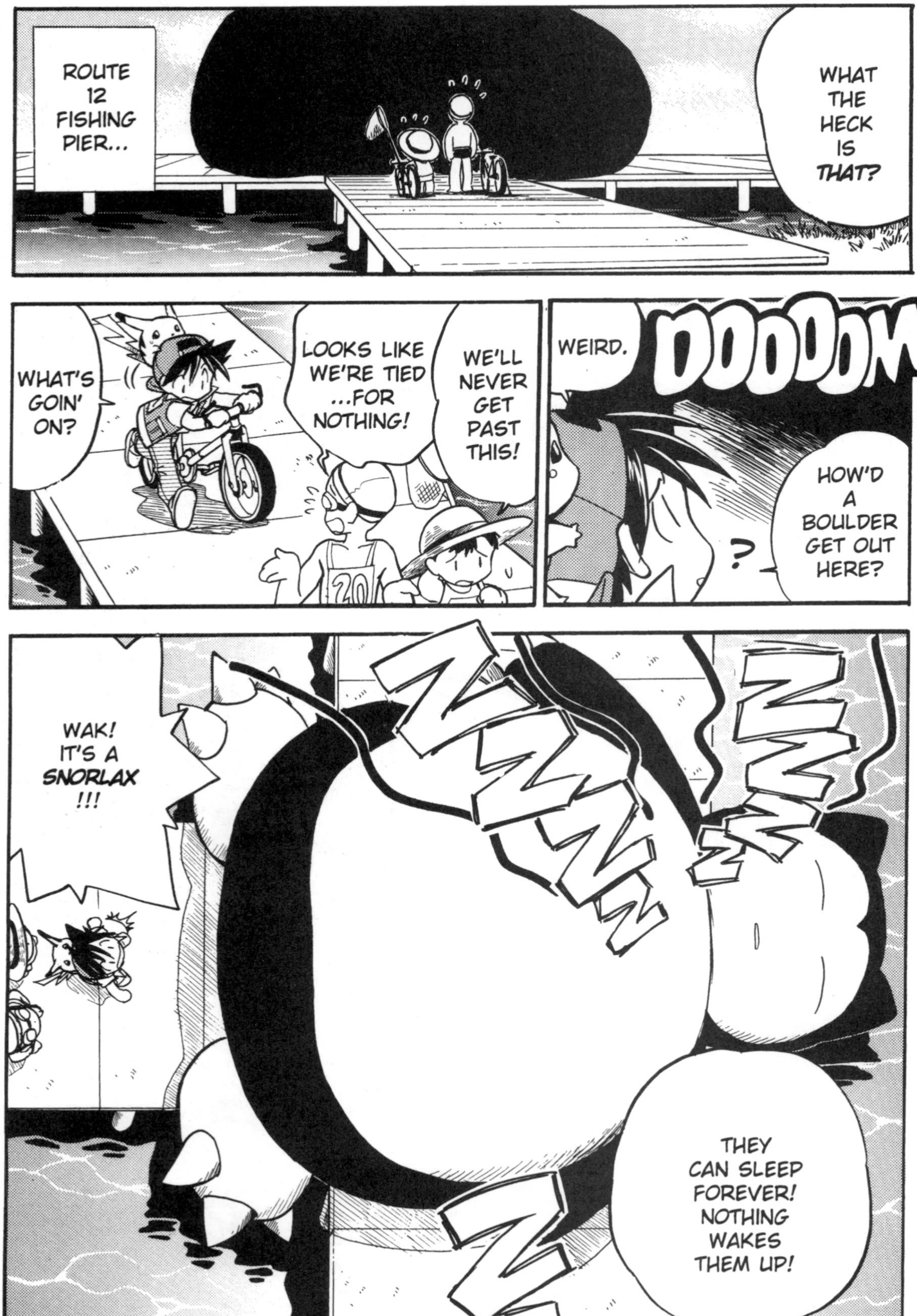
ROUTE 12 FISHING PIER...
WHAT THE HECK IS *THAT?*
WHAT'S GOIN' ON?
LOOKS LIKE WE'RE TIED ...FOR NOTHING!
WE'LL NEVER GET PAST THIS!
WEIRD.
DOOOOM
HOW'D A BOULDER GET OUT HERE?
?
WAK! IT'S A **SNORLAX** !!!
THEY CAN SLEEP FOREVER! NOTHING WAKES THEM UP!

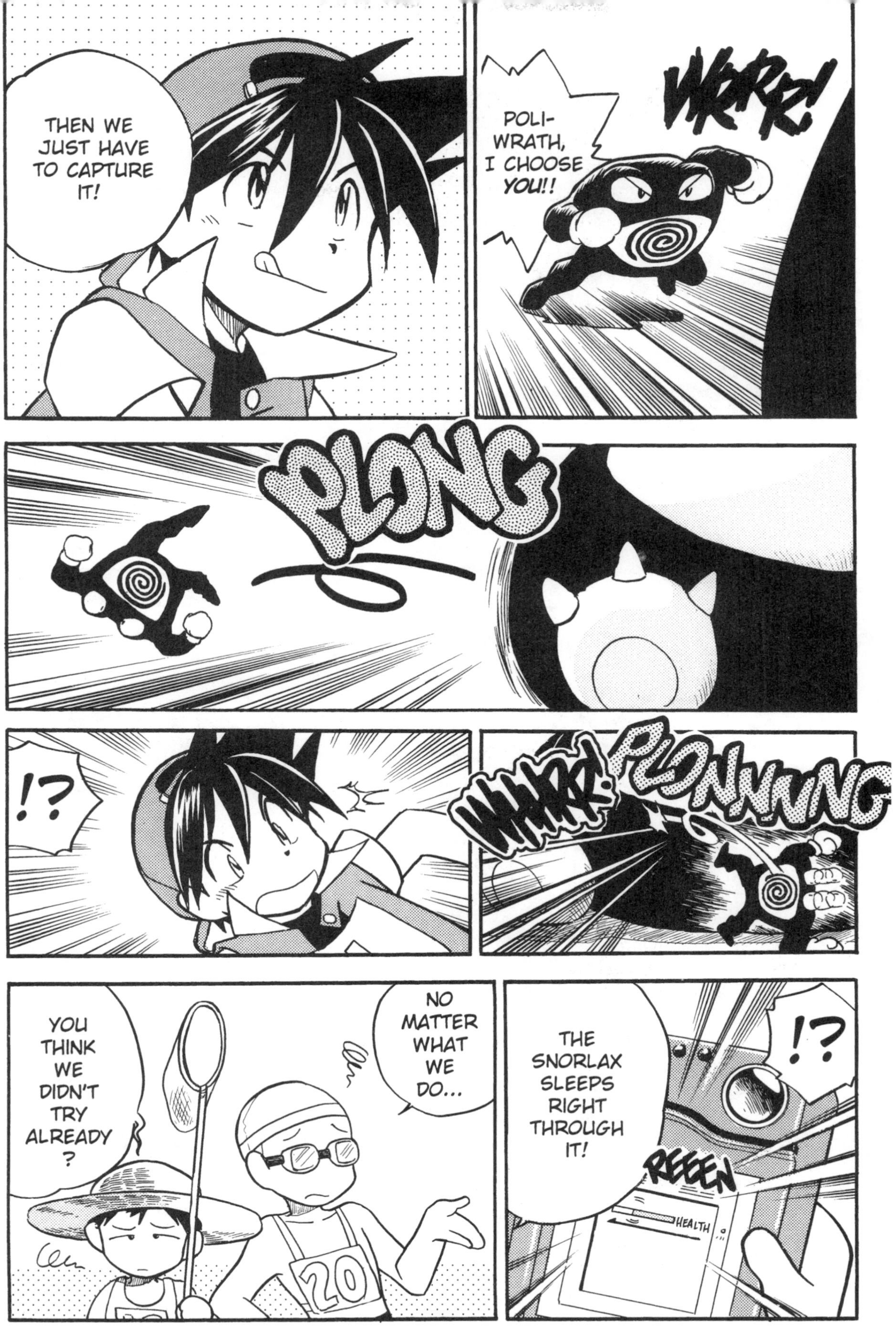
THEN WE JUST HAVE TO CAPTURE IT!
POLI-WRATH, I CHOOSE *YOU*!!
VWRRR!
PLONG
!?
WHIRR!
PLONNNNG
YOU THINK WE DIDN'T TRY ALREADY?
NO MATTER WHAT WE DO...
THE SNORLAX SLEEPS RIGHT THROUGH IT!
!?
REEEN
HEALTH

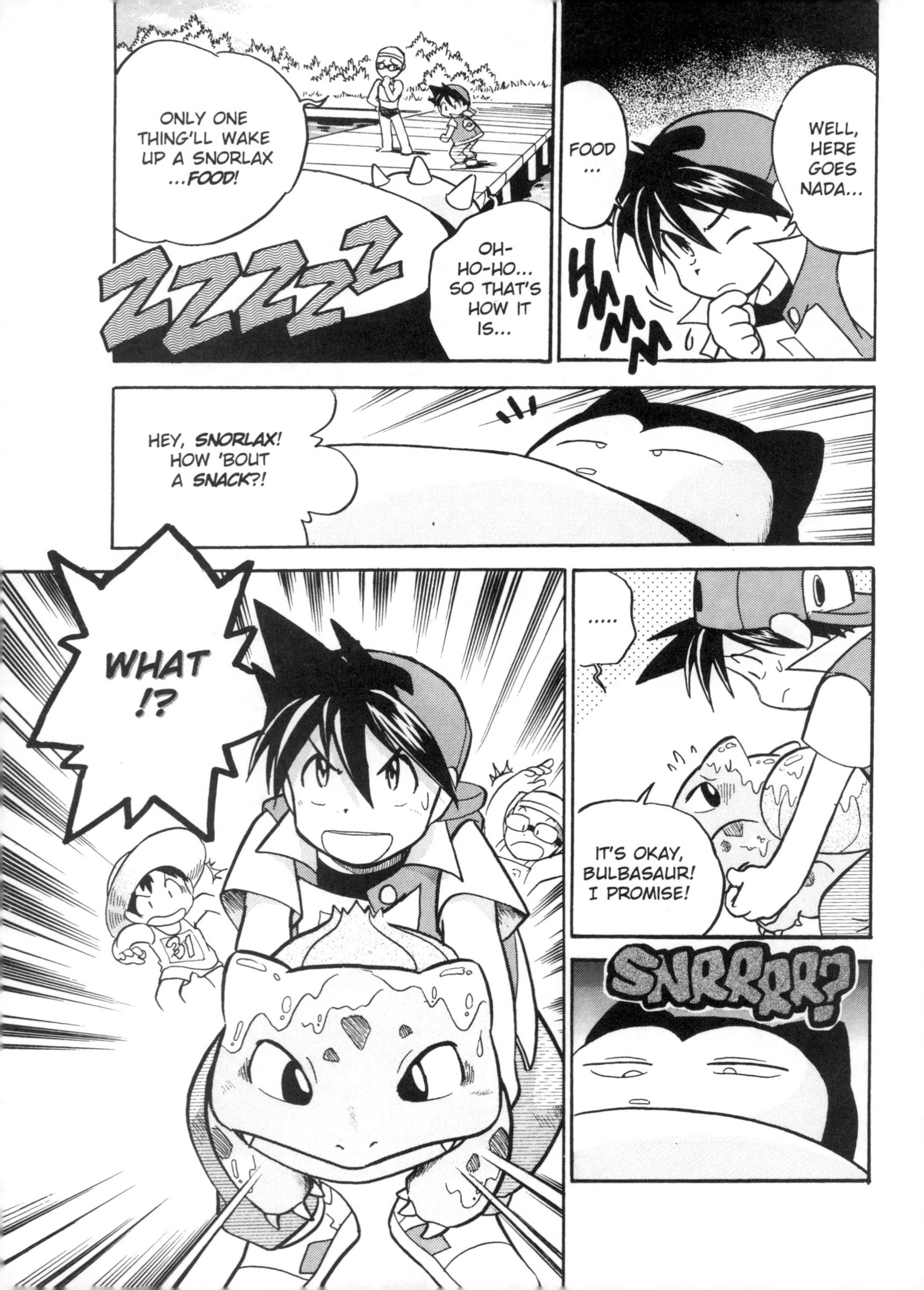
ONLY ONE THING'LL WAKE UP A SNORLAX ...FOOD!
ZZZZZZ
OH-HO-HO... SO THAT'S HOW IT IS...
FOOD ...
WELL, HERE GOES NADA...
HMMMM
HEY, SNORLAX! HOW 'BOUT A SNACK?!
WHAT !?
.....
IT'S OKAY, BULBASAUR! I PROMISE!
SNRRRR?

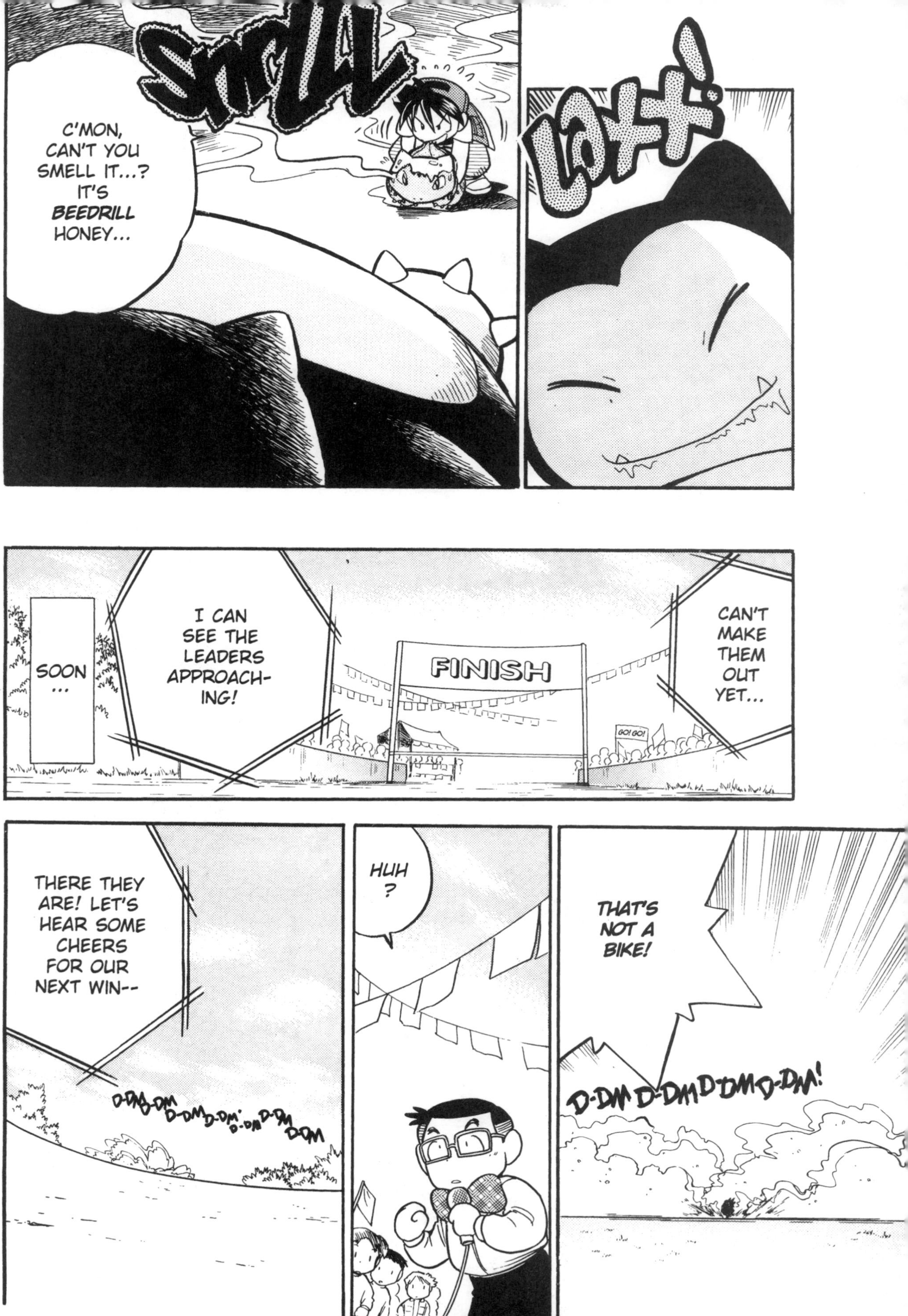
SMELL
C'MON, CAN'T YOU SMELL IT...? IT'S **BEEDRILL** HONEY...
SOON ...
I CAN SEE THE LEADERS APPROACH-ING!
FINISH
GO! GO!
CAN'T MAKE THEM OUT YET...
THERE THEY ARE! LET'S HEAR SOME CHEERS FOR OUR NEXT WIN--
D-DM D-DM D-DM D-DM D-DM D-DM D-DM
HUH ?
THAT'S NOT A BIKE!
D-DM D-DM D-DM D-DM!

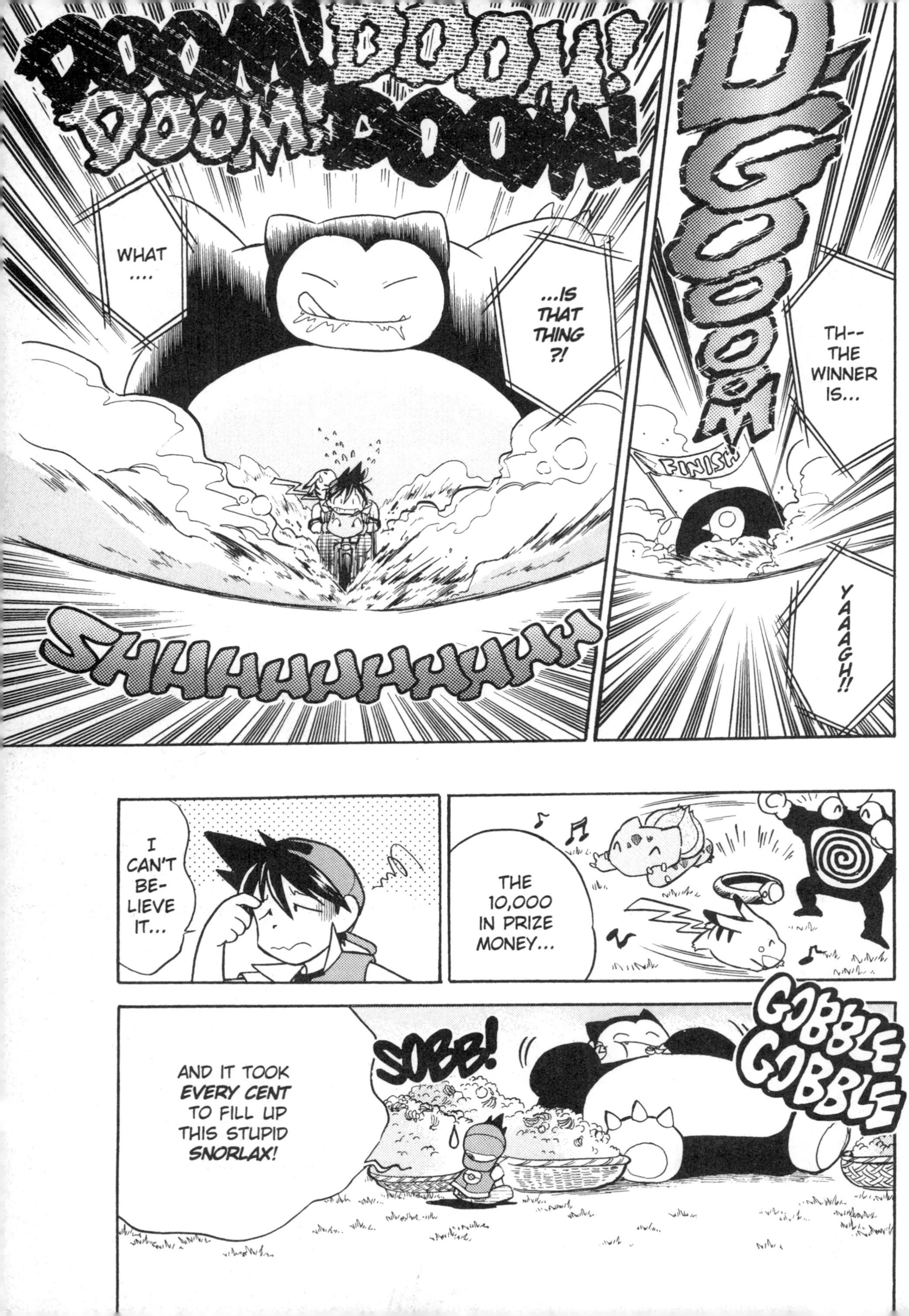
DOOM! DOOM!
DOOM! DOOM!
WHAT ....
...IS THAT THING ?!
SHHHHHHHHHHH
DGOOOOOOOM
TH-- THE WINNER IS...
FINISH
YAAAGH!!
I CAN'T BE-LIEVE IT...
THE 10,000 IN PRIZE MONEY...
AND IT TOOK EVERY CENT TO FILL UP THIS STUPID SNORLAX!
SOBB!
GOBBLE GOBBLE

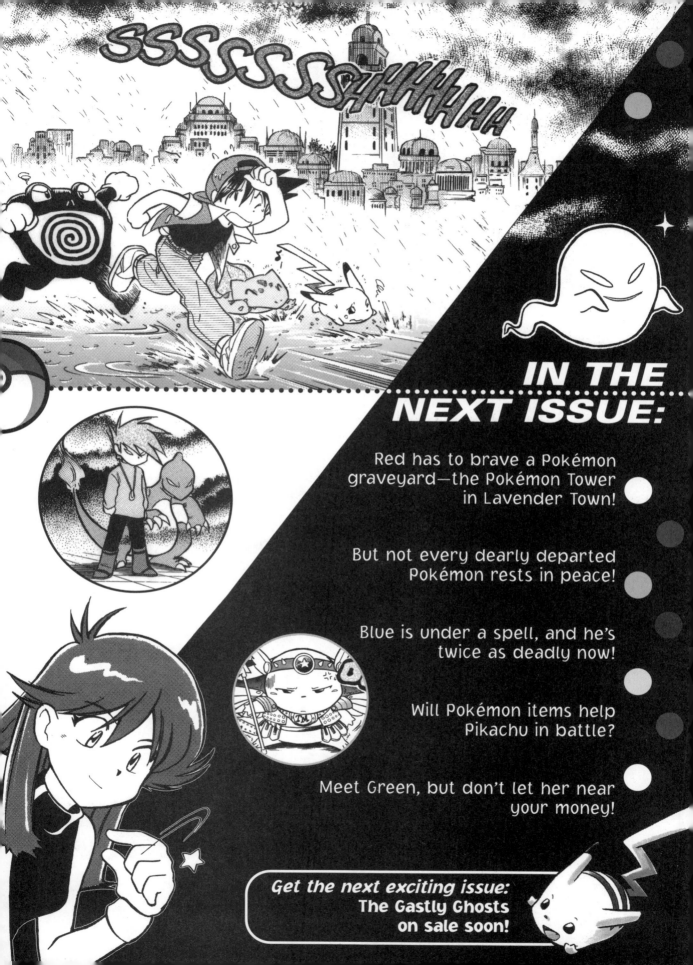

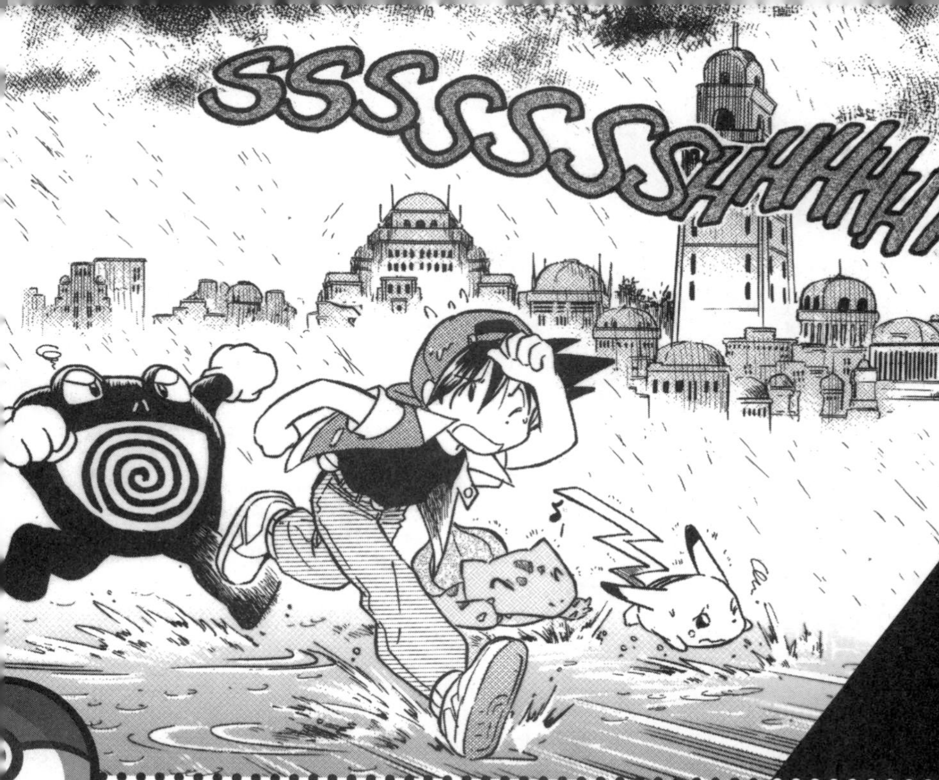
SSSSSSSHHHHHHHH

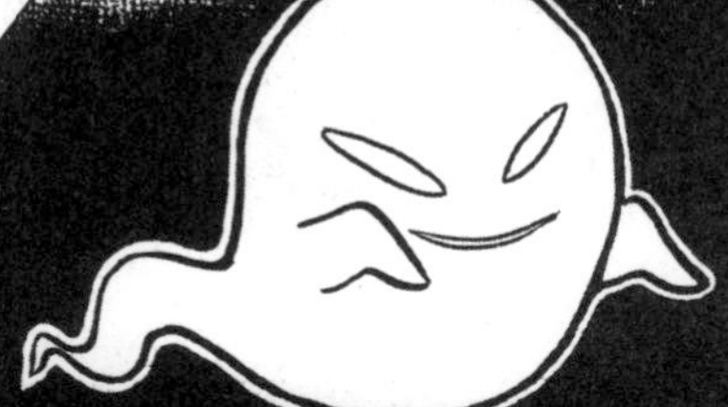

IN THE NEXT ISSUE:

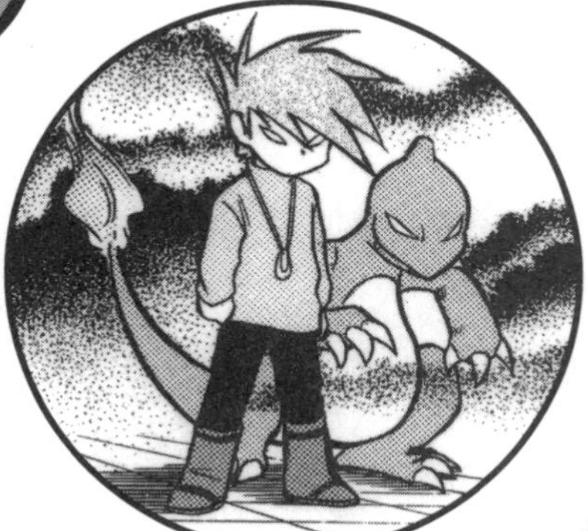

Red has to brave a Pokémon graveyard—the Pokémon Tower in Lavender Town!

But not every dearly departed Pokémon rests in peace!

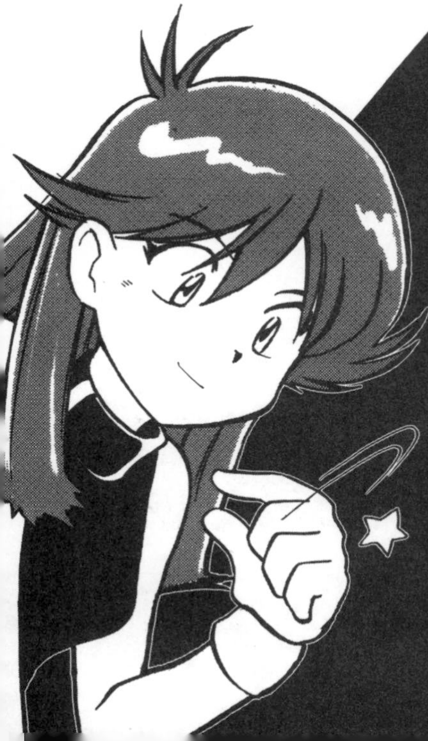

Blue is under a spell, and he's twice as deadly now!

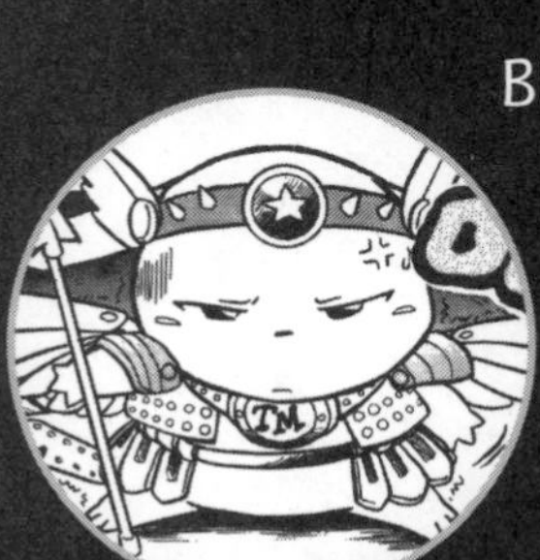

Will Pokémon items help Pikachu in battle?

Meet Green, but don't let her near your money!

Get the next exciting issue:
The Gastly Ghosts
on sale soon!

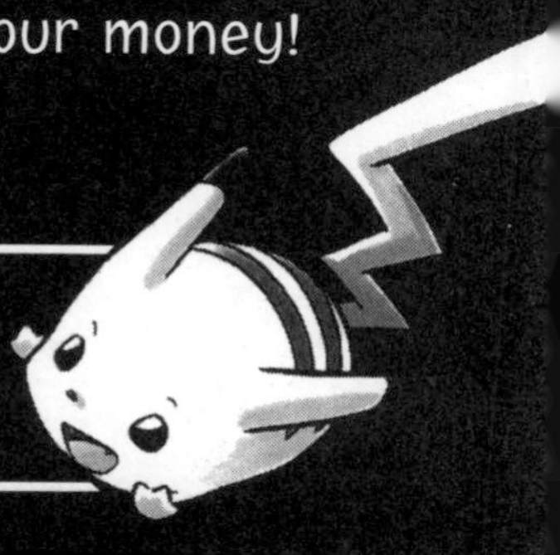

THE WORLD'S GREATEST FIGHTING TOURNAMENT IS HAPPENING...
TWICE A MONTH!

DRAGONBALL DRAGONBALL Z

story & art by
AKIRA TORIYAMA

32 pages each issue
$2.95 USA/$4.50 CAN

AS SEEN ON THE CARTOON NETWORK!

AWESOME MANGA ACTION!

The early, hilarious adventures of young Goku and his friends as they seek the Dragon Balls!

Goku's grown up & teams with his friends against the universe's deadliest villains!

©Bird Studio

The story of a boy who turns into a girl, a father who turns into a panda, and the weird Chinese curse that did it to 'em!

Rumiko Takahashi's Ranma 1/2

Ranma 1/2 ©1999 Rumiko Takahashi/Shogakukan, Inc.

Videos!

Four seasons of the anime TV series, plus movies and original animated videos. Available in English or in Japanese with English subtitles.

TITLE	ENGLISH	SUBTITLED
Original TV Series (Vols. 1-9)	$29.95 ea.	n/a
Collector's Edition TV Series (Vols. 1-6)	n/a	$34.95 ea.
Anything-Goes Martial Arts (Vols. 1-11)	$24.95 ea.	$29.95 ea.
Hard Battle (Vols. 1-12)	$24.95 ea.	$29.95 ea.
Outta Control (Vols. 1-12)	$24.95 ea.	Coming Soon
OAVs Vols. 1-6 (Vols. 1-3 are English-only)	$29.95 ea.	$29.95 ea.
Collector's Editions OAVs (Vols. 1-2)	n/a	$34.95 ea.
Video Jukebox	n/a	$14.95 ea.
Movie: Big Trouble in Nekonron, China	$34.95 ea.	$34.95 ea.
2nd Movie: Nihao My Concubine	$34.95 ea.	$34.95 ea.
Digital Dojo Box Set (9 Vols.)	$199.95 ea.	n/a
Anything-Goes Box Set (11 Vols.)	$199.95 ea.	n/a
OAV Box Set (6 Vols.)	$124.95 ea.	n/a
Hard Battle Box Set (12 Vols.)	$199.95 ea.	n/a

Plus!

Graphic Novels: 13 volumes & counting!

T-Shirts: 7 styles available in different sizes!

Music: 6 soundtracks from the anime TV series and movies.

Monthly Comics: Available by subscription or individual issues!

Merchandise: Baseball caps, Cappuccino mugs, watches, postcards & more!

AVAILABLE AT YOUR LOCAL COMICS STORE!
Or order online at WWW.J-POP.COM
PHONE: (800) 394-3042 • FAX: (415) 546-7086
CALL US FOR THE LATEST RANMA VIDEOS!

VIZ COMICS™

VIZ SHOP-BY-MAIL

GET YOUR FREE VIZ SHOP-BY-MAIL CATALOG!

ORDER NOW!

❊ PAYMENT IN US $ ONLY, PLEASE.
—Order by personal check, money order, or credit card. Visa/Mastercard accepted ($15.00 minimum for credit card orders). DO NOT SEND CASH!!
—With the exception of ANIMERICA, ANIMERICA EXTRA & PULP subscriptions, prices are for individual issues/videos only.
—Please allow 2-6 weeks for delivery.

❊ SHIPPING & HANDLING (included in price for Viz Comics subscriptions *only*)
(NOTE: 3 comic back issues = 1 item; 2 magazine back issues = 1 item.)

1. USA
Standard Service: First Class Mail
$4.00 1st item, $1.50 additional item
Express Service: 3-day service
$12.00 1st item, $2.00 additional item
❊ Include your phone number!
❊ We cannot ship Express to P.O. boxes!

2. Canada & Mexico
Standard Service: First Class Mail
$6.00 first item, $2.00 additional item
Express Service: Not available.

3. All other countries
Air Mail: Add 50% to your order

Make checks & money orders payable to:
VIZ SHOP-BY-MAIL
P.O. Box 77010
San Francisco, CA 94107
PHONE: (800) 394-3042
(have your VISA or MASTERCARD ready)
FAX: (415) 546-7086
(credit cards only)

BUY THESE PRODUCTS ONLINE AT www.j-pop.com!

If you order any of the titles listed below, include a signed, dated statement certifying that you are 18 years of age or older. Also include a photocopy of *one* of the following: driver's license, state I.D., *or* passport. Crying Freeman, Legend of Kamui, Lycanthrope Leo, Ogre Slayer, Pulp, Pulp Graphic Novels, Sanctuary.

(Catalog price listings — extensive tables of VIZ Comics, VIZ Video, VIZ Graphic Novels, VIZ Music, Cadence Books, Pokémon Books, Pulp, Animerica, Animerica Extra, Pulp Graphic Novels, and Merchandise titles with prices.)

ALSO AVAILABLE—GRAPHIC NOVELS, VIDEOS, MUSIC CD'S AND MERCHANDISE FROM

ISBN 1-56931-408

314

50595

9 781569 314081

7 82009 04953 1

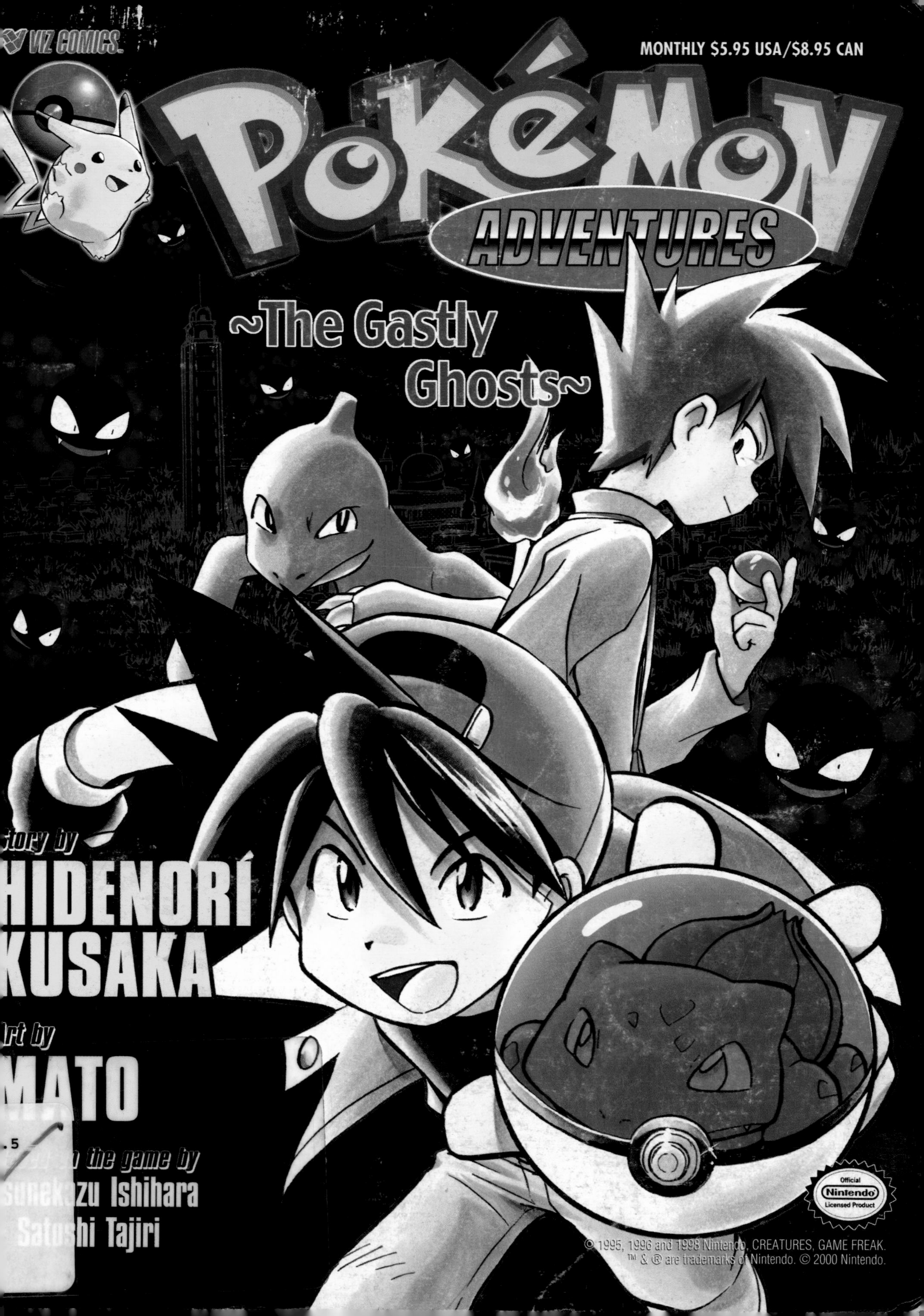
VIZ COMICS.
MONTHLY $5.95 USA/$8.95 CAN
POKÉMON
ADVENTURES
~The Gastly Ghosts~
tory by
HIDENORI KUSAKA
rt by
MATO
the game by
sunekazu Ishihara
Satoshi Tajiri
Official Nintendo Licensed Product
© 1995, 1996 and 1998 Nintendo, CREATURES, GAME FREAK.
™ & ® are trademarks of Nintendo. © 2000 Nintendo.